That Thing Between Your Ears

Is An Idea

How to get one. How to use it.
How to lose it when you're done.

Joe Anderson, *PhD*

***That thing between your ears is an Idea:
How to get one. How to use it.
How to lose it when you're done***

Print on Demand Version
Copyright © 2014 by Joseph V. Anderson
All illustrations in this work were created by the author, and are also protected by this copyright. All rights reserved. No part of this book may be reproduced, stored or transmitted in any form without permission in writing from the copyright owner.

Library of Congress Cataloging in Publication Data
Anderson, Joseph Vernon, 1950 –
That thing between your ears is an Idea
Joe Anderson, PhD
ISBN: 978-0-9847120-3-8

1. Business 2. Nonfiction 3. Management & Leadership
4. Self Help 5. Social Sciences 6. Professional & Education

Includes bibliographical references.

Cover Design by Jonathan Lee

For Susie, my favorite fan bather

Table of Contents

1. **The Fan** - The Difference Between Innovation & Creativity
2. **The Great ISM -** The Nuts & Bolts of Creativity
3. **Getting Off the Pot -** The Application Process
4. **Taking the Grand Leap -** Hurdling the Obstacles
5. **Brainfood -** Some Ideas You Better Master
6. **Open the Door** - The Art of Creative Thinking
7. **Jump Starting the Brain -** Some Tried & True Techniques
8. **Night Vision -** Learning to See in the Dark
9. **Dick Tracy, Where are you? -** Finding Patterns
10. **Life on a Leash -** Keeping Your Brain Under Control
11. **Doctor! Doctor! -** Curing Mental Block
12. **Standing in the Cow Pies -** Structure
13. **Six Easy Steps to Success -** How to Structure Creativity
14. **What About My Head -** Creativity & Personality
15. **Wall Vaulting -** It's Time to Leave the Nest

1
THE FAN
(THE DIFFERENCE BETWEEN INNOVATION & CREATIVITY)

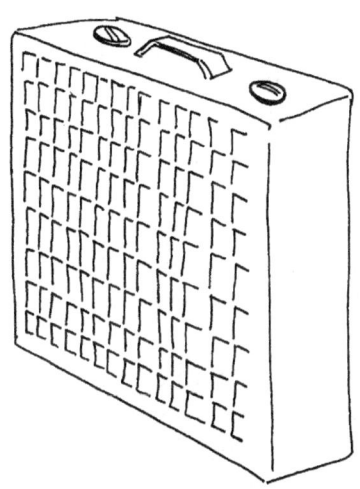

I was always a big fan of ideas. They solved problems. They opened up incredible opportunities. And they were just plain fun to come up with on the fly. In short – I looked at having an idea as an *event*. It was discrete, instantaneous and painless.

On the other hand, I never really liked *creativity*. It smacked of old ladies and doilies. The kind who "bathed" in the creative juices of a cluster of equals; contemplating consequences, discussing feelings and massaging their way to a conclusion at the pace of a snail. They took what should have been an event and buried it in *"process"*. Ick. Where's the fun in that?

Then life smacked me upside the head.

I took over an organization and stayed there for 10 years. It was on the brink of going under when I arrived, but it was a huge success by the time I left. And the glory belonged to "us", not to "me".

You see, _my_ flood of great ideas (those discrete, instantaneous and painless **events**) had dried to a trickle after the first 12 months. The only way we prospered was to invite in the old ladies (actually robust college women, in the full flush of feminist sensibilities). But I had the good sense to team them up with a bunch of jocks. It was glorious. Noisy. But glorious. We did process out the ying yang. And events popped constantly as well.

It turns out that you need **both** the process and the events to build and maintain a vibrant organization. Imagine that. Even the most 2-fisted executive has to slow things down a bit and bathe in those icky waters. You won't like it at first, but suck it up Bubba. The results are better than anything you'll come up with on your own.

You want a Great Idea? You gotta pay your dues. So _my_ advice is to cool your jets. I've got a story to tell you.

* * * * * * * * * * *

I used to keep a 20" box fan in my kitchen window, the kind with the plastic grills that prevent kids from sticking their fingers into the blade. It worked pretty well until the grill became caked with grime, at which point I discovered that old-fashioned family values are a matter of expediency. I was informed, with a smile, that fan cleaning was "man's work", and I set about conquering the task, grateful to know that modern feminism was alive and well. I unscrewed both grills and set them in the kitchen sink so that I could scrub them more comfortably. But I discovered a problem; I have a stubby finger. It wouldn't fit in between the grill slats, especially with a washcloth wrapped around it.

This would be a problem for most people. But I should point out that I hold a PhD, MBA, and a BA. Any man with that many initials after his name ought to be worth something. In addition, I have taught the art of creativity at some of the leading business schools in America. If anyone can find a top notch scrubbing solution ... it is me. And, in fact, I did pretty well.

I discovered that Q-tips do very well; and a good stiff bottle brush is wonderful, if you don't mind decorating the kitchen wall with fan crud. Then I remembered the airport shoe shine guy, and that gave me an even better idea. I slid a cloth through the grill and buffed. Not bad, but none of those methods hold a candle to the brainstorm my fertile mind experienced at that point. Quick. What tight place - full of nooks, crannies and crevices - do you clean each and every day? Yes! That's right! Your mouth! I was on a roll. I could feel the creative juices course throughout the very fiber of my being. I was hot. I was superb. And I was no fool, so I used my 7 year old son's toothbrush.

Within a mere 30 minutes I had ¼ of a grill so spit-polish clean that I could serve The President & First Lady on it. As I admired my work Susie walked into the kitchen and changed my pride to chagrin. She sized up the situation, delivered one of those pity-looks that only a wife can provide and, murmuring soft words of praise and assurance, she gently removed the grills from my care. She took them into the bathroom, tossed them into the bathtub and added a little detergent and water. Then she sat me down on the sofa and held my hands to control my urge to scrub something. Ten minutes later she ushered me into the bathroom, sprayed the grills with our shower massager and presented me with not one, but two, spotless fan grills. As I stood there with my credentials hanging out, I had one of those rare revelations that put a little sunshine in our lives. I had just witnessed the essence of creativity --- the art of vaulting the wall.

The Wall of Rationality
Most of us live within a "wall of rationality", which is a marvelous invention of civilization, made from the traditional wisdom concerning:
- what the world is like;
- how we ought to approach it;
- how situations are defined; and
- how one should go about addressing them.

In my particular case, the wall told me that: (a) the world is a dirty place; (b) I have a moral obligation to clean what I can; (c) scrubbing is the best way to clean; and (d) I should stretch my brain and discover the very best scrubbing technique. I unleashed myself within that wall, and I generated a flurry of activity. But I didn't have the foggiest notion of what existed on the other side of the wall, and that's why I didn't come up with the soaking technique myself.

Let's Compare Creativity & Innovation
In addition to making her over-educated husband look like a schmuck, Susie did something very important. She illustrated the difference between innovation and creativity, which is the core of all this talk about the wall of rationality.

I had been innovative. I had adopted a traditional definition of the problem --- ie --- dirt requires a scrubbing methodology. Then I built a very rational little wall around myself made from the bricks of what exactly scrubbing means. In my defense, I did pretty well. After all, I did discover a new use for the common toothbrush. I was very innovative and I pushed to the outer limits of the wall. But my accomplishments paled in comparison to Susie's.

Susie had been creative, rather than merely innovative. Instead of getting trapped inside the traditional wall of rationality, she vaulted it and ran into the great beyond. And there she built a new wall --- based on a completely different definition. She didn't see the problem as a scrubbing problem ... she redefined it as a soaking problem. After that it was easy.

Innovation sits Inside the wall.
Creativity roams the "great beyond."

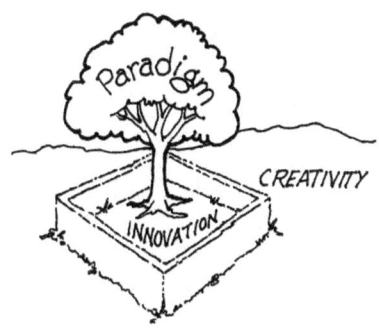

If you want to see the difference between innovation and creativity in its starkest form, consider this. Good solid innovation led me to a solution that would have taken 4 hours. Creativity led Susie to a 10 minute solution. When you think about your own business, your own life, your own relationships --- do you want to settle for innovation -- or would you like to have a little creativity?

A Closer Look At The Wall

Innovation is very nice. It follows the rules. It stays within the wall. It follows a very rational stream of if-then logic that uses knowledge, data and comparison to arrive at a defensible solution. It's neat and orderly, and managers adore it. But as time goes on, it becomes harder and harder to achieve a competitive advantage within that wall. A focus on quality and efficiency can help, eeking out every advantage that exists within the wall. They may even carry you to the interior face of the wall, where the Q-tips and toothbrushes grow. But a focus on quality and efficiency can't take you over the wall, because they are tied to the core definition (called the paradigm) which sits dead center within the wall, and the tether does not stretch any farther. Consequently, most people and firms spend their time on innovation rather than on creativity. And that's a shame because creativity is where the real breakthroughs and major profit potential exist.

In the Wall's Defense

I'm not one of those liberated free thinkers who believes that all walls, rules and structures are bad. So don't go out and trash the wall. The fact of the matter is that the wall of rationality in any given situation makes our world predictable and fair. Take the grocery store for instance. I hate standing in line. I also weigh well over 200 pounds and once had an offer to play football for the Chicago Bears. So, there's an obvious resolution for my impatience. But I have yet to do it. Why? Because I bump into the wall of rationality. I know that the checkout line is different than the line of scrimmage. And I know that creaming the old lady in front of me won't elicit the same cheers I used to get on the gridiron, unless she's got an irksome personality. You see, I know that the rules change from one situation to the next. And I know what those different rules are. I'm civilized. Which means the old ladies of the world can relax.

So when you get right down to it, the wall of rationality addresses the long term welfare of the group, and how each of us should behave within it. And for the most part, it serves us well. Consequently, we like to spend our time inside the wall, because it feels safe and secure.

Problems with the Wall

We spend most of our time inside the wall because we're trained to. That is the role of school, and I'm seeing it first hand with my son. He takes his fan encrudded mouth to second grade each day, and brings home a constant stream of stars and awards - for standing in line, for sharing, for being quiet and obedient - for staying within the wall. And though he envies the kid who discovers that crayons are also terrific projectiles, he applauds the classroom cop who nails that hot dog.

- ◆ Someone told Tom Edison's parents that he was retarded, because he wouldn't concentrate on 1+1=2.
- ◆ An art professor told Ted Gesell (later known as Dr. Seuss) that he couldn't draw, simply because his artwork looked odd.
- ◆ And little Albee Einstein was constantly in trouble because his hair violated the school dress code, as well as the law of gravity.

By the time most of us reach 3rd grade, the fear of God has combined with the adhesive stars and awards to firmly establish the wall. And once that happens it is nigh unto impossible to even imagine that anything exists beyond it. The world is flat all over again, and nothing exists beyond what we can see.

Then, after we're thoroughly socialized, we become adults and get a job with a firm that wants creativity, demands creativity, and rewards it. Whoops! We are utterly unprepared. So we scramble to find out how to do this wondrous thing, and in the process we are amazed to find out that survival and success actually depend on the very same things that got us through first grade:
- taking turns,
- coloring within the prescribed lines,
- being quiet and orderly,
- and above all others ... being obedient.

As it turns out, maybe school is a perfect preparation for what most of us confront on the job.

There is a wall. It may surround designing computers instead of using construction paper and paste, but it is a wall none-the-less. It sets out;
- what the world at XYZ company is like,
- how a good XYZer ought to approach it,
- how XYZ's problems and opportunities are defined, and
- how a good XYZ employee should go about addressing them.

The only thing that's really new is that there's also a set of stock excuses and scapegoats to explain why XYZ has once again been aced out of the market by some competitor from Japan, Bulgaria or Saskatchewan.

So, What's The Point?

1. **There is no universal wall of rationality** that governs all of existence. One of the things that makes life interesting is that we have a wall of rationality that surrounds every activity we do and every role we play. There's one for work. There's one for parenthood. There's one for courtship. And there's even a wall that governs scrubbing a fan. In truth, we tend to build a wall for each type of situation that we face.

2. **We are the masons**. To be sure, everyone else - including parents, teachers, bosses, politicians and spouses - tries to do it for us. But in the final analysis we build our own walls; actively, or by making a conscious decision to punt and use the walls that someone else has made for us. Either way, we have to come to the point of accepting our own responsibility. If you're old enough to read and understand this book, then you're old enough to accept your responsibility. It's part and parcel of being an adult.

Creativity In Business

As the Swiss painfully discovered, creativity is a crucial element in business. In fact, creativity can vanquish even the best innovations.

Time travel with me. Chicago, August of 1947. There were few things in life better than sitting at the local soda fountain with an ice-cold Coca Cola. Everything was white tile and light grey Formica. It radiated cool. And those glorious overhead fans created a breeze that made the city sweat and grime just float right off you, which is exactly why soda fountains were the #1 outlet for soft drinks at one time. And Coca Cola ruled the roost. The other 29 brands of cola didn't stand a chance; Coke kept adding new ways to handle and dispense cola, and new ways to serve it (fraps, frizzes, floats, swirls, etc.): in short – an innovation a week.

Then Alfred Steele read an article in <u>Popular Mechanics</u> or some such magazine, and turned Pepsi Cola from just one more no-name brand into the number one contender in 1948 by walking away from soda fountains. He handed Coke a virtual monopoly in the #1 retail channel of the day and instead used his meager resources to go after grocery stores with a vengeance. Coke laughed all the way to the bank – laughed, that is, until America performed its mass migration to the suburbs 18 months later. Suddenly America started buying its cola from an entirely new location – suburban grocery stores – and Pepsi had the shelf space locked up when Coke came knocking. And by 1958, America stopped going to soda fountains altogether – because they all had new fangled air conditioners hanging in their windows, and ice cold Pepsi in the fridge. Al had jumped the wall and run a deep post pattern in the meadow. You see, he'd read about Levitt Town and several other sub-urban housing projects. And he'd read about air conditioning too. Then he just put 2 and 2 together and took the enormous risk of betting the farm on his educated guess.

Creativity is the common thread running through all these examples. It is the source of competitive advantage, and therefore profits. It is also the thing that makes those examples memorable and gives us the "gee whiz" and "by golly" response as we read them. Creativity is the fuel that drives the engine of industry; finding new markets and ways to exploit old ones, developing new products and delivery systems, formulating new pricing and financing options, and addressing the needs and wants of buyers with data and images that touch the heart as well as the mind.

Yet a Presidential blue-ribbon commission published a very disturbing conclusion in the mid-80's. It said, unequivocally, that the U.S. economy was characterized as a vast sea of risk-averse mediocrity dotted infrequently with sparsely distributed islands of innovation.[1] Yikes! No wonder the Japanese were doing so well back in the 80's. They didn't have much competition.

In fact, they were kicking America's butt from one end of the marketplace to the other. They had taken a huge chunk of the auto market, obliterated the U.S. in electronics and were making enormous strides in every field they entered. The balance of trade flipped as US consumers clamored for Japanese goods – because they were better in every respect – better designed, better constructed, and sold at a cheaper price – despite being shipped all the way from Japan. Meanwhile, Jimmy Carter was running around the White House in a sweater, turning down thermostats and turning off lights. And the best we could do was demand that each other "buy American" so that …well, so that we could continue to churn out even more substandard stuff.

Things got so bad in fact, that Japanese officials felt secure enough to start taking pot shots. Akio Morita, the co-founder of Sony and co-author of <u>The Japan That Can Say No</u>, said "Real business entails adding value to things by adding knowledge to them, but America is steadily forgetting this. ... America no longer makes things, it only takes pleasure in making profits from moving money around."[2] When your competitors feel secure enough to be condescending, you know you've got a problem.

It's easy to criticize. The hard part is fixing the problem. This book is an attempt to do just that. So let's leave any further hand-wringing to those who have no idea where to go from here. Our focus will be on the future, and the past will enter primarily as a launch pad for taking the next step.

The Elusive Secret of Creativity

Jon Henderson, an executive at Hallmark, said, "You can't just order up a good idea or spend money to find one. You have to build a climate and give people the freedom to create things."[3] The central idea here is radical. It says you can't make creativity happen, no matter how much you reward or punish folks. Instead, the best you can do is to allow creativity to happen. That is a major frustration for two-fisted executives, but it is completely in line with the stream of reports that comes from "creatives" (those who create) from as far back as Michelangelo. The dominant theme from those sources is one of release, not imposition.

Michelangelo said he'd never really created a statue. He only got the gravel out of the way so that the statue inside could be released. Bach said much the same thing about music. Authors report the same phenomena, citing the muse within. Even inventors echo this message, from Thomas Edison to Paul MacCready, inventor of the first practical man-powered airplane and electric car. In fact, MacCready credited daydreaming as his major tool. It let him get underneath what he was *supposed* to think and find out what he really thought down deep in the shadows.[4] Now that was a man talking about vaulting the wall of rationality. But since he never bought this book, he had to come up with a different term --- letting go.

So, How Do You Let Go?

Relax. In essence, **that** is the essence. The creativity is locked inside and you have to relax and let it out, you can't snatch it out. Terrific, you say. We're losing market share. The competition's come out with yet another new model. My job's on the line because I can't think of anything to do. And some jerk from the ivory tower is screaming in my ear "RELAX! RELAX! RELAX!".

Yet the jerk keeps murmuring "relax" as though slumber is the secret of competitiveness. I'm the jerk. And the problem is that our vocabulary doesn't really have a better word for the desired state of being.

- ◆ Maybe it would help to think of a jogger. The body pumps, sweat cascades from pores, and there is a constant jarring of the body with every hoof beat. Yet the mind is relaxed, wafting languidly through the surroundings or in some intellectual playground.

- ◆ Or think about Orel Hershiser, the Dodger's pitching ace, who blissfully sang hymns to himself while he fanned one batter after another to win the World Series. That's "relax" ... the mind at peace in the midst of tremendous physical or intellectual exertion.

There is a difference, you see, between functional stress and emotional stress. Functional stress can actually invigorate us. Emotional stress wipes us out. Exercise puts tremendous stress on the body. But after a brief shower, most people feel alive and spunky for the rest of the day. Watching a fatal car accident requires little movement or thought. But afterwards we're so wiped out we need to lie down for a while.

One of the great all-time examples of relaxing in the eye of the storm has to be the 2004 Boston Red Sox - the ones who finally beat the Bambino's curse and won the World Series. The World Series itself was no big deal. They sailed through that in about 2 days time, obliterating whoever it was that represented the National League that year.

The storm was their playoff series with the fearsome New York Yankees – the bane of their existence and the crux of the Bambino's curse. For eighty years the Yanks had stood between Boston and the series. For eighty years the Sox had found a way to fold and die. And 2004 was no different. The Yankees had them on the ropes. The Sox were two games behind and one out from death.

And then it happened. One of those tipping point moments, when Fortune shifts her weight and everything starts going the other way. The New York fans went berserk. Cops in riot gear lined the foul lines to keep Hell in its bottle. And as the camera panned the Sox dug out you noticed that they were in a separate realm. They were having fun. In fact, they'd been having fun during the whole playoff series.

Orel Hershiser may have been in communion with the most high during his triumph. The Red Sox were in a more earthy communion with the beast of the clubhouse. And then Curt Shilling got out there on the mound, bleeding through his sock for 6 innings because --- well, gee whiz --- because that's what a guy does. It's fun to give one up for the Gipper. These guys weren't playing baseball; they were acting in a Jimmy Stewart movie. It was fun. They were relaxing. All they had to do was go out there and the director would make sure it all had a happy ending.

Meanwhile, the New York players were stressing out about doing things right. As a result, they wore themselves out and crashed and burned. And just to prove it wasn't a fluke, Boston repeated as world champs in 2007 – in the exact same fashion.

Where Do We Go From Here?
Look at what you've learned already.
- First, creativity is simply vaulting the wall of rationality.
- Second, creativity comes from individuals, not groups.
- Third, you are responsible for your own creativity.
- And finally, all you have to do is relax.

But that last one is easier said than done. Relaxing is very hard to do because trying to be creative is closer to car crashes than jogging for most people. The attempt creates so much emotional stress that dysfunction sets in. That's because creativity seems like such a mystical, and therefore daunting, task. Consequently, there is a need to de-mystify creativity and move it from the emotional to the functional realm. When that happens, relaxation has a chance. That's the purpose of this book. We're going to de-mystify creativity, starting with the very next chapter.
- We're going to make creativity seem so normal that it's no longer frightening.
- We're also going to hold up a mirror so you can see your own creative potential, which will boost your confidence.
- And we're going to give things names so you've got some hooks on which to hang ideas.

We're going to take a carving knife to creativity and dissect it. By the time we're done we'll know what creativity smells like, not just how to spell it. So, as my good friend Bill Shakespeare said, "Lay on MacDuff, and damned be him that first cries, 'Hold! Enough!'"

End Notes
1. *The report of the blue-ribbon Commission on Competitiveness was carried on the UPI wire service on February 14, 1985.*

2. *Akio Morita and Shintaro Ishihara, The Japan That Can Say No, Kobunsha Publishers, Tokyo, 1989. You can read an English review and excerpt in "A Japanese View: Why America Has Fallen Behind", Fortune, September 25, 1989, p. 52*

3. *Jay Cocks, "Let's Get Crazy", Time, June 11, 1990, p. 41*

4. *Leon Jaroff, "He Gives Wings to Dreams", Time, June 11, 1990, p. 52*

2
THE GREAT "ISM"
(THE NUTS AND BOLTS OF CREATIVITY)

Watch CNN. What you'll see played out before your eyes every single night is that the world is ruled, rocked and healed by "isms".

- ◆ Creation<u>ism</u> contends with Darwin<u>ism</u> for control of public schools.
- ◆ We've set up an entire government network to find sex<u>ism</u>, age<u>ism</u> and rac<u>ism</u> under every bed because we no longer have commun<u>ism</u> hiding under there to frighten and entertain us.
- ◆ We watch national<u>ism</u> turn Rwanda, Yugoslavia and Chechnya into pools of blood and genocide,
- ◆ and we wish to goodness that everyone would just choose bapt<u>ism</u> and capital<u>ism</u> so that we could all get a good night's sleep
- ◆ ... as long as we don't experience nightmares about liberal<u>ism</u> or social<u>ism</u>.

And then we awaken to the "Today" show where some dweebish scholar tells us that last night's bomb attack simply illustrated the ongoing battle between Romantic<u>ism</u> and Rational<u>ism</u>, which is, of course, the engine that drives terror<u>ism</u>.

Enter the <u>Great ISM</u>

We are surrounded by isms. They are the energy that propels civilization towards its own future. And if we want to determine whether that future will be prosperity or the poorhouse, we need to tap into the one great ism that is the foundation for all the rest. Its name is ISM, somewhat like giving your name as "I am the great I AM", which tips us off that this is a concept of Biblical proportions. And yet, like most great concepts, it is simplicity itself.

The <u>Great ISM</u> stands for
* *Invention*
* *Synthesis*
* *Modification*,

the 3 ways that creativity expresses itself.

1. **Invention** is the activity we usually think of when someone says creativity. It is the act of making something out of nothing. With fervid apologies to physicists and their theory of atomic displacement, it <u>is</u> possible to make something out of nothing. Beethoven faced a blank page and made the immortal 5th symphony spring to life. Shakespeare did the same with <u>Othello</u> and a host of other masterpieces. The Wright brothers filled an empty sky with planes. Without the <u>things</u> that come from invention, we'd still be living in caves.

However, don't lose sight of the fact that it is also possible to invent an <u>idea</u>. Someone invented the idea of freedom. And someone else invented the ideas of exchange, democracy, home and family. And someone else invented the word "invent". Think about that for a moment. An airplane is meaningless unless someone first invents the idea of flight, and the words and numbers to express it. Wow. In that case, the greatest inventor of all time was probably the person who invented the first word. It was probably a noun; something like "food". Up until that moment <u>nobody</u> knew what he wanted. Everything was confusion. After that moment, <u>everybody</u> knew what he wanted. It worked so well, we invented a word for everything and the world changed. That's why the book of John in the New Testament begins, "In the beginning was the Word, and the Word was with God, and the Word <u>was</u> God." It was trying to say that God (Jehovah, Yahweh, I AM) was the great inventor of all of life. Now that's what you call staking a claim.

Anyway, invention is without question a form of creativity. **But it is not the only form**, nor is it even the most important one. There are others of equal import - which is crucial to remember - because most creative people are <u>not</u> inventors.

2. **Synthesis** is the act of relating two or more previously unrelated phenomena. Take a cake. Take a shovel. Put them side by side and stare at them. Boom! The cake server is born. It's a miniature shovel. That's synthesis.

The first wheel was the product of invention. So was the first axle and the first box. But until someone came along and synthesized them into the cart, mankind didn't get much good out of the three components. Synthesis is the core of society's advancement. Invention is nice, but synthesis is the real engine of survival and prosperity. Have you ever performed synthesis? Have you ever filled a balloon with water instead of air? Now there's a very gratifying bit of creativity, especially when performed on a 4th floor balcony. Have you ever used a carpenter's chisel to separate frozen hamburger patties? Have you ever found that a beach was more conducive to reading than a library? If so, congratulations. YOU synthesized. And that puts you in the same league as Thomas Edison. He never created anything in his whole life. All he did was suck the brains of others and synthesized like crazy. So whadayathink? Are you creative?

3. **Modification** is the act of altering something that already exists so that it can: (a) perform its function better, (b) perform a new function, (c) perform in a different setting, or (d) be used by someone new.

Putting pontoons on an airplane doesn't change the function of the plane (take off, fly, land), but it certainly broadens the settings in which it can perform its function.

Moving a hose to the back end of a vacuum cleaner changes the whole function of the machine, from sucking to blowing.

And something as simple as lowering a water fountain, or adding a footstool opens its use to a whole new group - unattended children. The most ambitious modification effort of all time might just be the effort to rebuild and re-inhabit New Orleans after Hurricane Katrina hit in 2005. Unless you count rebuilding Haiti after the earthquake of 2010.

The <u>Great ISM</u> is impure

Invention, synthesis and modification are the crux of creativity. But they do not exist in isolation. Instead, they overlap so much that it is difficult to separate them in reality. In fact, we are hard pressed to find any examples of pure invention beyond the creation story in the first few chapters of <u>The Bible</u>. And even there, Eve came from Adam's rib, a marvelous by-product of synthesis and modification. Creativity, therefore, is best envisioned as a bubbling stew in which the various components lose their crisp separate identities and start to meld into an interwoven whole.

This is a crucial point, because it affects our self-confidence and the goals we feel we must meet before we accept ourselves as being creative. You don't have to invent in order to be creative. In fact, our most prolific inventor wasn't really an inventor. Thomas Edison merely synthesized and modified existing items. Vacuum bulbs had been around for a century: So had burnable filaments. And electricity had been the subject of scientific inquiry for half a millennium. All Tom did was put it all together. I don't know about you, but realizing this fact makes me feel a lot better. I don't have to be God to be creative. All I have to be is a conscientious version of me. In fact, I can accomplish a lot in this life just living off of my ability to modify things, like Sinbad did.

Sinbad and the Cave of Torture

Sinbad, the sailor of myth and legend, was held captive by the evil sorcerer-king. After a period of unspeakable torture, the king came to him with a riddle that would determine his ultimate fate.

"See, here." said the king. "I have a parchment with nine spots. Your life depends on how you use them. I want you to connect them all with as few lines as possible. The lines must be straight. And each line must touch another, as though a hand had made them all without leaving the page.

"If it takes you five lines or more," said the king, "I shall leave you in this living hell of daily torture. Four lines buys you a speedy and painless death. Three buys your freedom. And if you do the impossible, and use only two, you win my kingdom, the hand of my daughter, and I shall become your prisoner."

Sinbad pondered a moment, carefully folded the parchment several times, then stabbed it with a stick. "There, my Lord", said Sinbad. "Nine spots with a single line. And the price for it is your head."

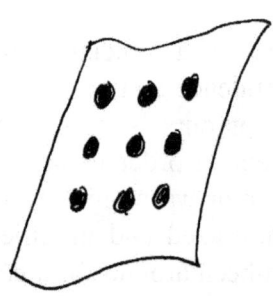

The king let out a fearful scream of disbelief, then realizing that his own riddle had doomed him, he ripped off his head with his bare hands and gave it to Sinbad before collapsing. Sinbad of course, took the daughter, the treasure and the kingdom and lived in sumptuous wealth to a ripe old age. Modification, you see, can be as creative and as useful as invention.

The Creative Eye

Creativity is how Sinbad got a head. As you can see, bad puns often hold great truths. The fact is that many folks spend their entire lives in the cave of torture, because they simply do not see the opportunities that sit in their laps. They deny themselves their own creativity by imposing even more constraints on themselves than the natural order or an evil king ever imagined, such as:

- the paper must remain flat,
- we can't diminish or increase the size of the dots,
- we have to use a standard size writing instrument,
- all the constraints are equally important, or
- we can't go outside the apparent boundaries.

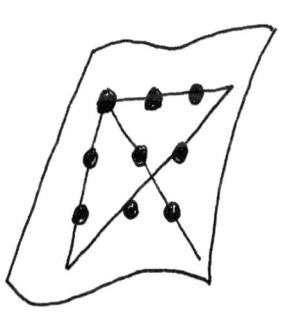

The last one is a major cause of creative blindness. Take another look at the piece of parchment. When we first look at it, we imagine that the outer dots form a fence, and all our efforts must remain tortuously inside. But if we do that, 5 lines is the best we can do.

It is only when we go *outside* that self imposed boundary that we arrive at the 4 line solution

That's creativity, literally going beyond the boundaries. And things get even more interesting when you try to do it with one line. As it turns out, Sinbad didn't have the only good solution. In fact you may want to try your own before you proceed.

How would you connect the dots with one straight line?

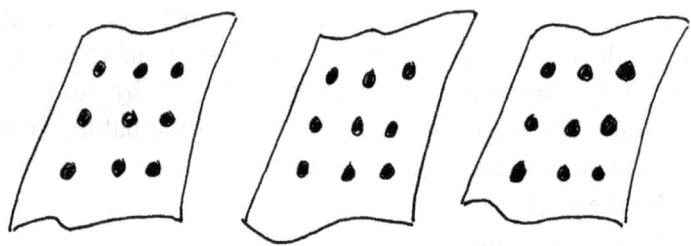

I hate these kind of brain teasers. If it were me, I'd give up on logical solutions. I'd get frustrated and start doing stupid stuff. Give it a try. Sometimes stupid is good therapy.

Go on …… you know you want to.

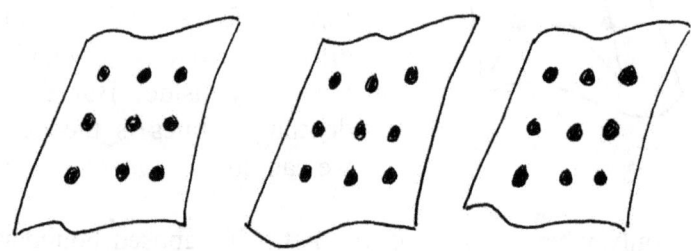

Now, let's take a look at some solutions.

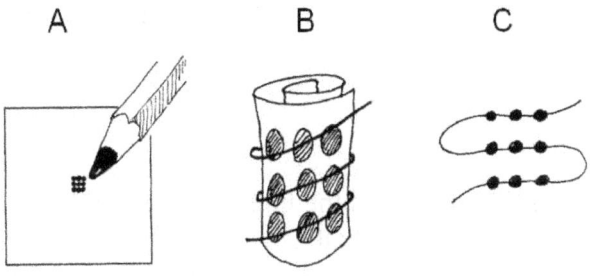

Solution A changes the environment. Go to a copier and set it on "reduce". Then keep re-running the parchment until the 9 dots essentially merge into 1 dot. Then your #2 Ticonderoga will "connect" them in 1 line. Or get a gigantic magic marker. Same net effect.

Solution B goes a step further. In addition to changing the size of the dots (this time making them gigantic) it also changes the contour of the page - from flat to cylindrical. Once you've done those two things, one line will circle the tube and go through all 9 dots, if you pick the right angle. And finally ...

Solution C illustrates an important point. If the core task (connecting the dots with 1 line) is important enough, violating one or more of the constraints may be the proper solution. We simply remove a constraint and use a curved line. Pretty simple, and effective.

All of this gives rise to several observations.
1. Creativity involves navigating between and among the constraints and opportunities established by the environment.

2. We tend to see even more constraints (boundaries) than really exist.

3. There is wide latitude within the boundaries.

4. Sometimes creativity involves changing or violating the boundaries themselves.

Seeing Relationships

Creativity is a matter of seeing new relationships, like finding a fruit that guards the house, is incredibly loyal and plops itself into your cereal bowl. Al Capp invented just such a creature back in 1948 in his comic strip "Li'l Abner". It was called a Shmoo.

The precise description of a Shmoo is "...the lovable creature [that] laid eggs, gave milk and died of sheer esctasy when looked at with hunger. The Shmoo loved to be eaten and tasted like any food desired. Anything that delighted people delighted a Shmoo. Fry a Shmoo and it came out chicken. Broil it and it came out steak. Shmoo eyes made terrific suspender buttons. The hide of the Shmoo, if cut thin, made fine leather and, if cut thick, made the best lumber. Shmoo whiskers made splendid toothpicks. The Shmoo satisfied all the world's wants. You could never run out of Shmoon (plural of Shmoo) because they multiplied at such an incredible rate. The Shmoo believed that the only way to happiness was to bring happiness to others." The schmoo was <u>the</u> number 1 merchandising phenomena of the early fifties, featured in "Lil Abner" the leading newspaper cartoon series of its day (60 million readers per day). Just about 50% of the entire US population were Shmoo fans! (Source: http://www.al-capp-lil-abner.com)

Is that a bit odd? Yes. Unreasonable? Nope, the Shmoo was just new and shocking, because it appeared to violate the laws of nature, including those about animated phalluses.

But wait a minute. The laws of nature are merely boundaries. They're just one more wall of rationality. And they've been vaulted before.

The laws of physics tell us that one body cannot occupy two places at the same time. Well, the essence of that law was violated thousands of years ago, with the first letter. One's thoughts could be in Athens, and in Corinth, at the same time. And if we take Descartes at his word, "I think, therefore, I am", (cogito ergo sum) – an ancient author simultaneously existed in both places, since his thoughts did.

Here's an interesting thought. I moved in with you the moment you opened this book. What's for dinner?

The telephone and live TV are simply better violations of the same law, because the thoughts are truly simultaneous whereas the letter writer had probably forgotten the thought by the time it got to Corinth. In order for letters, phones, telegraphs, and TV's to be invented someone had to believe that the laws of nature could, in effect, be broken. And one of the biggies is the definition of "place." It used to be <u>static</u>. I had to get home before I turned on the tube or made a call. The cell phone made "place" <u>dynamic</u>. Place is wherever I, and my phone, happen to be at the moment.

What About You?
So now we've established the concept of creativity. It is the Great ISM; which requires both insight and action. Do you

recognize it? Probably so. But the big question is, have you experienced it in your own life? Do you know what it feels like? In short, are <u>you</u> creative?

Most of us say "no" because we've never done anything big with it. We've never written a symphony, much less a hit song. We've never painted the Sistine Chapel, much less our own house. We never really invented anything. So we're likely to sit back and content ourselves with identifying creativity rather than practicing it. That makes us as useless as a drama critic ... all talk and no action.

The fact of the matter is we've all been creative. Most of us just missed that fact because we never labeled our behavior as such. And that's because we didn't understand the various types of creativity. Remember, creativity is nothing more than vaulting the wall. Composing a symphony certainly qualifies. But so does inventing the automobile, and much to our surprise, so does rearranging office furniture to improve work flow. Creativity exists to the same degree in all three ventures. And that's a point we often miss. The action determines the existence of creativity, not the fame and fortune that might follow it.

So far we've done two important things.

1. We've established that creativity has three aspects: Invention, Synthesis and Modification.

2. We've also established that you trigger creativity by relaxing one or more of the constraints imposed by the Wall of Rationality you currently inhabit.

So congratulations, you are now willing to consider life beyond the wall.

Stop the presses for a minute!

I just had an insight ... I was wrong about Edison. He <u>was</u> creative. Very creative. He was a master of synthesis and modification. He just wasn't inventive, in the literal sense. And I have fallen into the same trap I've been trying to get you out of. Isn't that a kick? I could rewrite these first few chapters to hide my faux pas, but I think I'll just leave them as is. Maybe it'll illustrate the creative process, which moves ahead in fits and starts. Besides, it has literally taken me 15 years to get from the prior paragraph to this one, and I'd like to have something to show for all that time. This is it.

The difference between Edison and Einstein is locale.

They were both creative, perhaps equally so. They just chose to use that creativity in different locales – Einstein on the mountain top, Edison in the trenches. This one simple observation has just opened my eyes, and everything which follows is a result of this one little epiphany. Here's my brain teaser for you ----- once you step beyond the wall, where do you want to go?

Let's do a quick quiz
How do you want to use this tool called creativity?
- ◆ Do you want to exploit the current system in which you find yourself, or do you want to change it?
- ◆ What drives you: the quest for wealth and glory, or the welfare of mankind?
- ◆ Are you looking for one good idea, or a whole new way to think?

- Do you need things to be concrete, or are you happy as a clam with mushy thought?
- What counts as long term for you: a month or a century?
- Is there such a thing as ultimate truth?
- Would you know it if you saw it?

Your answers to these kinds of questions will tell you where to go once you step outside the wall. And for the sake of simplicity, let's consider just two options:

1. you can work on the mountain top, or
2. you can work in the trenches.

Life on the mountain top is ambiguous. You've got your head in the clouds most of the time. Everything is theoretical: the nature of man, the purpose of governance, the essence of matter, the vagaries of the human heart. You search for the next big thing. You do that primarily by practicing the invention aspect of creativity, with inevitable help from the synthesis aspect.

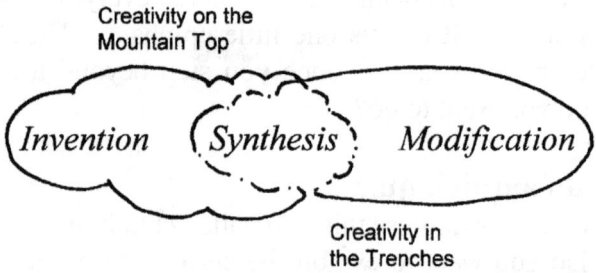

Life in the trenches is a different story. Jack Welsh will regale you with the stories of General Electric, Bill Gates will join you and Steven Jobs for a lively discussion on the relative merits of brilliance and doggedness, to which Edison will offer his 90% retort (it's 90% perspiration).

And you will dedicate yourself to great ideas that'll grab an extra 6% of market share, decrease turnover, or raise the test scores of your 8th grade class 9 points. And where will you get those great ideas? Most of them will be from the modification aspect, but the real breakthroughs will come from synthesis. Pure invention, however, does not generally live in the trenches. It prefers the rarified air of the mountain top.

The bulk of life is lived in the trenches, not on the mountain top. But if some of us weren't up there taking on the big issues, the rest of us would soon run out of new things to do down here in the trenches.

So the mountain and the trench are inextricably tied together. Therefore, any reasonable book about creativity needs to address life at both locales. The question, of course, is how to do it.

> The most popular approach to this problem is to pretend it doesn't exist. You declare that the world is simple, and then focus on one little corner of life in the trenches. These are the books that read like a Ginsu Knife ad. Breathless, upbeat, singsong – "Life is simple, just follow these 3 easy steps to guaranteed success --- but wait! There's more! You also get the 4 pillars, and this attractively wrapped home version of the 8 commandments of prosperity. Just call ………." You get the picture.

> Another approach is to try to lump both locales into the same pot and try to come up with a few general rules that make sense out of the stew that results. I tried this approach myself, for 15 years. It doesn't work. Too complex.

So you are left with the only other option. You write a separate book for each locale. One book for creativity on the mountain top, and a separate one for creativity in the trenches. And that's just what I did. This one is on Creativity in the Trenches. The other one is on Creativity on the Mountain Top.

3
GETTING OFF THE POT
(THE APPLICATION PROCESS)

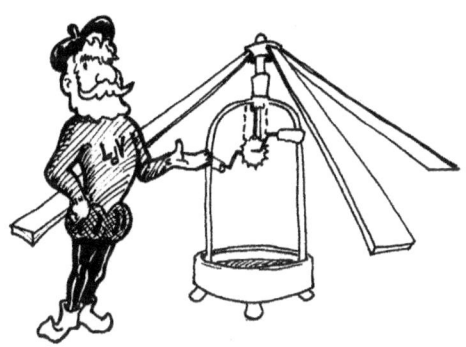

When you're down in the trenches, ideas without <u>applications</u> are nothing more than creative constipation. The ideas just pile up inside and become a pain. That's why the last chapter ended with a call to action.

We need to focus on getting the ideas out where they can do some good. The Wright Brothers made their first flight in 1903, and a mere 66 years later we landed a man on the moon. But here's a point to ponder - Leonardo da Vinci actually invented the helicopter back in 1492 - the same year Columbus discovered the new world - and we still have his parchment drawings to prove it. But he doesn't get credit as the father of flight because he never got around to the applications phase. He never built a working model of the darn thing. Just think about that for a minute. If he'd done so, the world might be entirely different:
- ◆ the first manned flight might have occurred in 1493;
- ◆ the first jet in 1535;
- ◆ the first space shot in 1547; and
- ◆ the first moon landing in 1556.

That would have all occurred before the first white settlement on Plymouth Rock actually occurred, in 1602. And given mankind's history of colonization and migration, half of the human population would now be spread across Mars, the moon and other planets outside the solar system.

But he <u>didn't</u> do it. It was therefore an idea that went nowhere ... because da Vinci the Great, lacked courage. So mankind had to wait 450 years until the Wright Brothers came along and finally succeeded, not because they were bright, but because they were <u>brave</u>.

Wow! It feels good to preach a little. Everything's so crisp and clear in sermons. And we always know who the bad guy is. The problem, however, is that sermons suffer from over-simplification. That's why they're so persuasive. It's also why they're not much good for learning anything. So give me a minute here and I'll crawl off my soap box and start over.

"Ideas by themselves have limited value. They have to be applied to some specific problem before society receives any benefit. And that is why we ended the previous chapter with a call to action. However, that action must be seen within the context of contemporary technology and culture. Leonardo da Vinci didn't have access to carbon steel, or internal combustion engines, or vulcanized rubber for gaskets, belts and tires. He didn't even have access to a good laser driven tool and die shop. So let's not be too hard on him." (There. The calm approach may lack the color of personal slurs, but it makes up for that by adding a little insight.)

Leonardo da Vinci didn't get to be "the father of flight" because the technology of 1492 couldn't match the sophistication of his ideas. He also missed out on the glory because an Italian sailor stole his headlines that year ... by discovering the other side of the World. And that caused every government in Europe to throw their resources into shipbuilding, which killed the funding for blue sky ideas like da Vinci's.

But still, I am haunted by the "what if" conundrum. If only da Vinci had tried. He was a bright guy. He could have jerry-rigged something. And if only he had, I really believe that the world would have been different. We wouldn't really have gotten to the moon by 1556, because there is a limit to what the technology of an era can do. But a moon landing by 1800 might not have been out of the question.

You see, the prototype, itself, may be the most important contribution. When it appears, the rest of the world wakes up and takes notice. Then other folks jump on the bandwagon, bring along new technologies, and take the idea far beyond the imagination of the original inventor. Old Orville and Wilbur Wright would probably be baffled and terrified by the Space Shuttle. But without them the shuttle might never have occurred. A prototype, any prototype, creates an anchor for other inventions, industries and people that do not even exist yet. And therein lies the great paradox of creativity:

♦ **The idea, itself, is an individual accomplishment;**
♦ **but the application is usually a group effort.**

Consequently, if you want to be a well rounded creative person, you have to be functionally ambidextrous. On the one hand, you have to be able to thrive on your own out there in the meadow. And on the other hand, you also have to work with the immigrants who are attracted to the new wall you build out there.

The Application Process

If making ideas come to life were easy, you wouldn't need a book like this, would you? You'd just kick back and wish them into existence ... from drawing board to marketplace in an instant. The problem is, application is actually a fairly complex ritual; usually involving five major components.

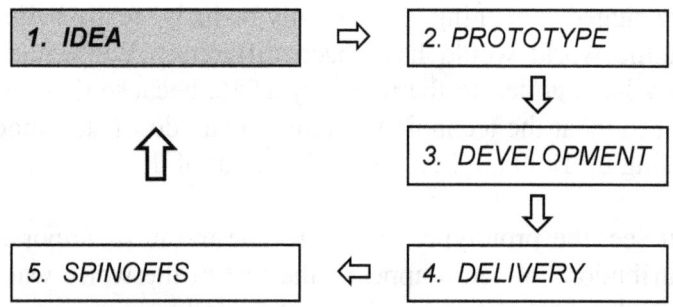

The Idea

"Say, I've got an idea. Let's use steam to make things move." That simple thought was the birth of the industrial revolution, because the steam engine was literally the engine that drove the entire thing. The problem was that

the world was in the birthing room for over 1,500 years on that one. Back in 100 B.C. the wealthier Romans had steam heat pumped into their houses and, in the process, they discovered that steam made things move. But they never saw a use beyond entertaining the kids by making pinwheels spin. It wasn't until 1495 that Leonardo da Vinci himself came up with the specific ideas and drawings for a working steam engine. So, we've got to clarify things a bit and differentiate between a <u>general idea</u> (gee, steam can make things move), and a <u>specific idea</u> (Hmmm, we could make a thing called a locomotive with it). And the thing to remember is that each specific idea has a ton of little general ideas behind it.

* * * * * * *

Hmmm, I bet fire would make things hot.
Hmmm, I bet water is one of those things.
Oops, tossing water directly on the fire doesn't quite do it.
Hmmm, I think I need something as a barrier between the fire and the water.
Oops, a flat surface doesn't do it. The fire still goes out.
Hmmm, maybe a concave object would be better.

Why don't I call it a pot.
Look, Mabel. The water dances. Yikes! The gods are angry.
They're making a cloud on the pot.
What? I made the cloud? No kidding?
Hmmm. That means I get to name it. Let's call it Stan.
What? You think it sounds stupid? Ok, you name it then.
Steam? What kind of a name is that?
Look, Mabel. That bay leaf you tried to throw into the pot just wafted off into the sky. My steam cloud makes things move.
Hmmm, I wonder if steam would make other things move.
Look! Putting a funnel on the pot makes the steam stronger.
It sent your bay leaf 20 feet into the air. That's 10 feet more than your old record. That makes me the... what the heck?
My funnel just blew off. I better invent bolts.

Mabel, why did you put dirt in Johnnie's wagon?
And why did you make the fire on top of the dirt?
What? it's a portable stove? Great, just what we need.
Mabel, this damn portable stove doesn't work right.
Look, I bumped it and my funnel pot tipped sideways. How're we going to ....
Oh my God! It moved! The damn thing's crawling away.
Go get master da Vinci! Maybe he can find a way to kill it!

* * * * * * * *

Obviously, those little general ideas are as important as the big specific one, because without the one, you never get to the other. That's why Bell Labs was established with a charge to its scientists to have fun, rather than an edict to invent something useful.

And *that's* why the nation supports the abstract research of academia.

They're trying to generate the <u>general</u> ideas that will lead to bigger and better <u>specific</u> ideas in future generations. So the next time a goober-mouthed, aw-shucks politician tries to make points by whipping the academic geeks, see if *his* hot air can be funneled into something useful. Honest to god, I am sick of politicians who proudly make stupidity a national policy.

A second point here is a personal one. You should be proud, as well as dedicated, if your gift is having those little <u>general</u> ideas. They'll add up to something big one of these days. Old Mabel and what's-his-name were absolutely crucial to the steam engine, even if da Vinci gets the glory.

And a third point is that da Vinci really does deserve the glory. Old Mabel and what's-his-name were just futzing around outside their hovel, entertaining themselves. Leonardo, however, was the one who combined that stream of general ideas into a cohesive whole and applied all that knowledge to a <u>specific</u> functional purpose. So even though both types of ideas are important, ***the specific idea is the thing that gets the world moving.***

The Prototype
Leonardo bumped into the same problem with the steam engine that he had with the helicopter. The current technology just wasn't advanced enough to make a prototype. Metal work hadn't advanced beyond making

swords and body armor, so there was nothing strong enough to contain the steam until it worked up the strength to do anything more than blow around bay leaves. That had to wait until mankind perfected making cannons - which gave old James Watt the know-how to make the first commercially viable steam engine in 1776. So Watt, not da Vinci, goes down in history as the inventor.

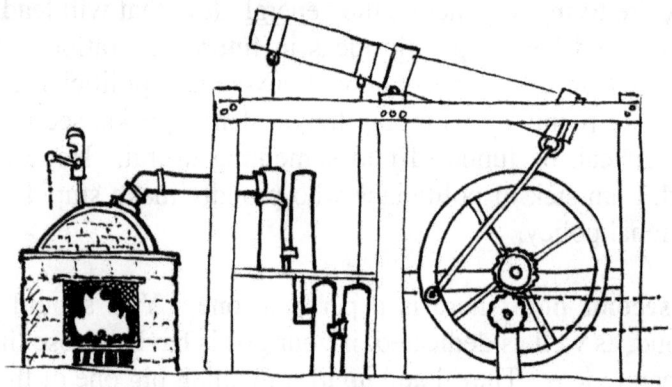

If you want glory, aim at making prototypes. And don't feel bad for the Mabels and Leonardos that may get left in the dust, because the prototype does deserve the glory. It gives tangible expression to the idea. It lets other people comprehend the idea. And it proves to everyone else that the idea is doable and, therefore, worth their time and effort. So get ready for company.

"Failure is an orphan. But success has many fathers."

Actually, success resembles one long paternity suit. No one was willing to crawl the wall and attach themselves to your idea while it was an unproven commodity that might fail. But success with the prototype changes all that. Folks come out of the woodwork and they're all willing to share the credit, or at least bask in the glory. The problem is, they don't come as disciples. They each think they're the prophet. So things are going to change in that nice little retreat you built out in the meadow. It'll become a beehive of contending egos and visions as you move into the realm of development.

Development

It's one thing to build the prototype. It's another thing entirely to work the bugs out of the system and develop the new and improved versions that can actually be used by other people. You'll need an array of new gauges, valves, piping, heating elements, boilers, plating etc. - all the things that are necessary to get a truly usable new product.

Development, you see, focuses on details rather than grand visions, and since no one (not even Edison or da Vinci) is a genius on all the details, you'll need the help of those folks who are ready to share your glory. And at that point, creativity becomes a group activity rather than the effort of one lone visionary.

Development relies on teamwork, structure and other organizational trappings. As a result, by the time creativity enters this stage, it travels in the guise of normal life.

In fact, development work gets extremely "normal". Most of the folks who get involved will be technicians, with a high level of formal education or mechanical expertise. And technicians are notorious for setting up a systematic process of perfecting the idea via testing and empiricism, rather than a random process based on revelation and insight. Science therefore replaces art as the chief mode of operation and a second wave of technicians is brought in, just to keep records for the first wave of technicians.

Pretty soon, you've got people everywhere you look. You can't remember all their names. But they'll need to eat, so you'll need a payroll, and someone to take care of it. And then you'll need to add salesmen, because without them there won't be anything coming in to feed the payroll. On and on it goes. Once you move beyond the prototype stage, life will never be the same. From that point on, creativity usually requires the kind of time, expertise and resources that only a group such as a firm, industry or government can muster. Consequently, it is the development stage that first ties creativity to issues such as management, politics and governance as well as macro economics.

Obviously, a different set of skills becomes necessary once you get beyond the prototype stage. The emphasis shifts from being creative yourself, to managing (stimulating and coordinating) the creativity of others. But that's a topic for another book, not this one. Of course, I just happen to be writing that book as well, so keep an eye on your local bookstore in the future.

Delivery

Delivery is the point at which the idea finally becomes useful. It translates into a specific machine, or process or institution that materially affects the function of the world. Watt may have invented the prototype steam engine in 1765. But it wasn't until 20 years later, in 1785 that a tremendous amount of development work led to the first working steam engine in a textile mill.

Delivery involves far more than simply dropping off the invention on the user's door step. Gas lights were a marvelous invention, but without laying an extensive system of gas pipes they would have been useless. They also required the development of an entirely new class of civic employees (lamplighters), and the manufacture of safety fixtures for the home. It was a very complex venture. And it was a money mill, creating thousands of jobs and giving the nation's economy a much needed boost.

Then the whole multi-million dollar network was rendered obsolete and useless within a single generation ... because Edison came up with his nifty little light bulb. Then Edison had to go through the whole rigmarole too. He had to build a large central generator, lay a grid of electric cable across the city, and build lamp fixtures before anyone could use that little bulb. Ditto for Alexander Graham Bell and his telephone. And the cycle repeats itself endlessly.
- ◆ The wonder resides in the prototype.
- ◆ The application comes from the development stage.
- ◆ But the usefulness comes from delivery. Not glamorous; but without it, the best idea is ultimately worthless.

A final point is this. Delivery is the ultimate group undertaking. One person can have the idea. He usually needs an assistant to build the prototype. Development pulls in dozens of people. But that pales in comparison to delivery, which often depends on hundreds or even thousands of people. Someone, after all, has to dig the trenches, lay the wire, and make all the deliveries. And I can guarandamntee you that it wasn't Tom Edison, Alexander Graham Bell, or even old James Watt himself. They hired gophers by the score. And at that point there was no avoiding the necessity of the extended and formal organization.

Spinoffs
The first useful steam engine began running a textile mill in 1785. Within 20 years, steam was everywhere.

Steamboats, steam shovels, steam tractors, and steam presses were sprouting up all over the world. And in 1804 the first steam engine chugged down a railroad track, ushering mankind into the age of modern transportation. Each of these inventions had their own trail of ideas, prototypes, development and delivery. But they were accomplished much faster than the initial steam engine because they were essentially spinoffs of the same idea, steam compression.

That one prototype opened the flood gates for a mind numbing array of new products, which takes us back to the <u>Great ISM</u> we covered in Chapter 2, because most spinoffs are the result of someone else's synthesis or modification of your marvelous invention.

- At this point we can see that creativity becomes an endless "do-loop" which feeds off itself.
- Each spinoff is actually a new idea, with a new prototype, development and delivery;
- that will lead to yet another round of ideas, prototypes etc. etc.,
- in which the specific idea that fueled one project becomes one of the many general ideas that fuel the next big specific idea.

"Hmmm, Mabel. Maybe this here radioactive glow could replace light bulbs in the future. By jingo, I feel another spinoff coming on ..."

Looking at the Gun and Target

Creativity is the gun. Application is the target. When you take a look at the chart (called "The Creativity Matrix), you might be surprised to see how the two fit together. They are completely meshed. Each stage in the applications process can be driven by any and all of the three types of creativity. The idea might be an invention, like the first steam engine. Or it might be a synthesis, like the locomotive, which was nothing more than the combination of the steam engine and the hand-pushed rail carts used in coal mining. Or the idea might be a modification, like moving from a 2-stroke to a 4-stroke engine.

And so it goes through each and every stage of the application process. Creativity in one form or another is actively at work bringing an idea from the confines of your fertile mind to the plates, garages or closets of the buyers. And that creativity is equally "big" and equally important, regardless of the stage and regardless of the type of creativity it is.

THE CREATIVITY MATRIX

	INVENTION	SYNTHESIS	MODIFICATION
IDEA	Aha! I betcha steam could do some useful work around here	Let's put steam and wheels together. OK. Now let's put steam together with a shovel	Lemme see. If I used explosions instead of combustion the piston would do double duty. It would be its own boiler!
PROTO-TYPE	The first boiler. Ain't she pretty?	Ah ... I call this contraption a steam shovel. How do you like it?	Lookee here. I think I'll call this thing a horse-less carriage.
DEVELOP-MENT	I need some kind of pressure gauge. Maybe Fred could figure it out.	This thing needs wheels or I can't move it. Hey, Fred was working on something he called a cater-pillar track.	Rats. The piston keeps blowing out every 200 miles. Call Fred. He can fix anything.
DELIV-ERY	Hmmm. Unless I lay some track this baby's not going anywhere.	I need to stock-pile coal near the worksite or this thing will die. I got it! I'll invent Service stations!	Shoot. I need paved roads or this thing will bog down in the mud
SPIN-OFFS	Hmmm. I bet steam could also run one heck of a shovel, too.	You know, if I burned gas instead of coal I could do away with the boiler.	Road building would sure be easier if ...I got it! Let's make a bulldozer

Take another look at the Creativity Matrix. There are 15 different spots where you can be creative. And all of them are important. So if you're sitting around feeling uncreative because you've never invented an idea, take a look at the matrix and then give yourself a loving kick in the shorts. Inventing an idea is just 1/15th (that's 7%) of the creativity matrix. That still leaves 93% of the creativity matrix staring you in the face. Now think hard.

- ◆ Have you ever decided that paper clips were great toothpicks? That's a spinoff based on synthesis. And your dentist congratulates you.
- ◆ Have you ever rearranged the groceries in your pantry so that meal preparation would be easier? Congratulations, you practiced modification in the delivery stage.
- ◆ Have you ever suggested a change in an advertising campaign that would address a whole new market? Congratulations, that's modification in the development stage.

You see? Tell me you see. Humor me. You're creative. You are. It's just sitting there inside you. I know it. And now you know it, too. All you have to do is admit it. Just look in the mirror and say, "By golly, I'm creative." If you admit that simple fact to yourself, you'll relax enough to let the creativity start to blossom.

End Note
The historical information on steam and other technology was taken from one of the more interesting books I've encountered: The People's Chronology, by James Trager (Holt, Rinehart, Winston, 1979).

4
TAKING THE GRAND LEAP
(HURDLING THE OBSTACLES TO CREATIVITY)

A.C. Markkula had a nice life. As marketing manager for Intel Corporation - the well known semi-conductor manufacturer - he had an interesting job, a cushy salary, and the recognition of his peers at conferences and conventions. Then one day in 1977 he opened his door and there stood Steve, a scruffy looking flake, who'd dropped out of college, flirted with "fruitarianism" and Hare Krishna, and spent a year in India contemplating his navel and the ultimate verities. Now Steve was storming back into reality with the claim that he'd discovered a bona fide wizard, plus a secret of the universe. He'd sold his VW bus for $1,300 and set up a venture to spread a special form of information across the globe and, said Steve, he'd chosen Markkula to be his special agent. All Markkula had to do was quit his job, hand over a quarter of a million dollars, and get to work. And though Markkula wouldn't get paid, he'd have the right to be an equal partner in the venture. Sounds like a great opportunity, huh?

Taking the Grand Leap
Well Markkula took it - that grand leap of faith that carried him beyond the boundaries of vocation, family and logic. That's how he hooked up with Steve Jobs and met the world's bonafide wizard, Stephen Wozniak. Markkula had just joined Apple, which still operated out of Wozniak's garage. He changed all that rather quickly. His first target was the capital market. He got a paltry line of credit from Bank of America to gain credibility and then raised $3 million from Venrock Associates (the Rockefeller family) and John Rock, a leading venture capitalist. With that money in hand, Markkula got down to business.

Up until 1977, the major market for personal computers had been hobbyists who derived more pleasure from assembling high-tech kits than using the end result for anything specific. Markkula decided to ignore those folks and charged after the plethora of small businesses who couldn't afford IBM's mainframe computers. He got a booth at a business trade show and spent 84% of the previous year's gross sales on advertising. Things took off and sales jumped to $774,000.

In 1978, Apple got IT&T to serve as its international distributor. It also expanded into the home market, but with a twist - the computer would be sold as a serious tool for budgeting, tax preparation and the like, not as a platform for video games. Dick Cavett, the cerebral TV personality, became the pitchman and Apple sold America on the PC as a user-friendly home necessity. In the process, Markkula found that TV advertising was also a marvelous way to tap the small business market. So the Cavett ads killed two birds with one stone and sales jumped 915%, to $15 million.

In 1979 Markkula simply did not have the money for the rapid expansion that was needed. Thirty other companies had entered the PC market and IBM was making noises about throwing its gargantuan resources into the fray. Markkula figured that Apple had 18 months to establish itself as a major player or financial ruin lay ahead. He had things to do, and no time to handle the sales function. So he contracted the services of 5 independent distributors and got out of the business of selling direct to his retail customers. It worked. Sales jumped 510%, to $70 million, and Apple took over as the undisputed market leader.

Then in 1980, Markkula reversed field. He dumped the independent distributors after less than a year and set up his own network of distribution centers. The independents had served their purpose and Markkula wanted the control, the profits and the dedication that come from a company-owned network. Sales hit $200 million, and Apple decided to go public. It's phenomenal sales figures "mysteriously" leaked out in the first week of December and on December 12 it floated $97 million in stock which was inhaled by the market. As an equal partner, Markkula had become a multimillionaire, in less than 4 short years.[1]

The Roadblocks
Boy! Talk about a nice example of everything we've discussed so far. The Apple story is it.

- ◆ It's got the PC itself, which was a synthesis of existing technology, and Wozniak's version, which was a modification.
- ◆ It's got grand leaps of faith all over the place, especially by Jobs and Markkula.

- It's got brilliant insights on market opportunities, bold open field running through the distribution system, and shrewd manipulation of investors.
- And it's got wealth and glory at the end of the rainbow.

This is what creativity looks like. But where did Markkula get all that creativity? He got it from the same place that you can get yours. It's hiding right behind the obstacles you've been nurturing so carefully.

Think about your own life. Are you as creative as you'd like to be? Are you as creative as you could be? Why not? In general, the list of reasons is fairly short. Creativity gets lost in the shuffle because people:
1. really don't know what it is;
2. don't want to be creative;
3. don't know how to get there; or
4. aren't allowed to be creative.

DON'T KNOW IT - One of the reasons why people have difficulty finding their way to creativity is because they don't know "where" it is. They don't know what it feels like when they get there. No one labels it for them so they can pass right through it without knowing, and consequently, they don't know how to return to it either.

When my daughter Amy was 8, we took her snow skiing for the first time. She had a horrendous time. The speed upset her, the lack of full control frightened her, and falling down made her frustrated. Then Mom did something crucial. She said "Amy, this is fun. The speed is fun. The wobbling is fun. Even the falling is fun. This, Amy, is what fun feels like." I realized what catharsis looks like as I watched her face. "Ohhhh," came the response. And the tears gave way to that grin of derring-do that frightens parents. Someone labeled the experience for her. Now she can find fun anytime she wants. **This book is an attempt to do the same thing for creativity. That way, when it nibbles at your toes, you'll recognize it and pitch your tent.** Amy now finds her joy by swimming with sharks; literally. She's a scuba diver. So now Susie sits around whimpering.

DON'T WANT IT - Alexis de Tocqueville, writing back in 1802, unwittingly put his finger on the American dilemma with creativity. He called it the tyranny of the majority, and noted that Americans suffer from it more than any other nation. We don't like oddity. We snub those who've got it, and we fear contracting it ourselves. So we buy our clothes, cars, houses and appliances according to prevailing fashion. Ditto for thoughts and behaviors. Political correctness currently dominates the stage. Smoking is out. Recycling is in. Individualism is out. Multiculturalism is in. And woe to the person who goes against the norms. We like our clothes a little spiffier, our cars a little shinier, our houses a little cleaner, and our politics a little more insightful than our neighbors. But that's about it - not different, just a tad better. We'd like to be at the top of the heap, not separate from the heap. We want to peek over the wall of rationality, but most of us fear actually being on the other side of it. More than anything else, we want to be like others. And down in our guts we know that creativity sets us apart. Too far apart. Creativity is frightening.

This book is a courage pill.
We'll try to make peace with creativity
and take comfort in oddity.

DON'T KNOW HOW TO GET THERE - I sat in the office of a major telecommunications firm and counseled an executive we'll call "Axel". He was enraged. He'd spent several million dollars revamping the organization. He'd sent every vice president and product manager to a two-week seminar on managing innovation. He even attended the seminar himself, and read every self-help book he could find. But nothing, absolutely nothing, happened. "I couldn't get a new idea out of a paper bag if the directions were printed on the bottom", he stormed. "I know the seven steps, the six rules and the four @#$%^! pillars. But when I sit down to think - nothing."

Axel is a classic case, a little rich in vocabulary, but classic none-the-less. Here was a man who knew what creativity was and could do. He was also a man who was clearly committed to doing it on a grand scale. But he couldn't even pull it off in his own life, because he didn't know how to get there.

He wanted to push a button, just like on a phone or computer. Push a button, get an idea - simple, clean and quick. Consequently, he got suckered by every step, rule and pillar peddler who came by. They were selling him what he wanted to hear, <u>not</u> what he desperately needed to hear, which was the truth. I gave it to him, and now I will share it with you.

You can't get there by pushing a button. You can't get there by memorizing a rule or a step, or by climbing a pillar, no matter how nice the view. There's only one way to get there. It's on the other side of the wall, and it doesn't much matter how you get over. Forget the formulas. Creativity is not a nice progression of logical steps. It is a mushy process. And **you get there more by feel than by conscious deliberate actions**.

Axel swore at me when I told him all this. But he was just desperate enough to let me stay. And just desperate enough to wade through the material that ended up in this book. "Well ..." you ask. "Did it work?" Let me put it this way, old "Axel" became one of the movers and shakers of the industry and ended up with his picture on the cover of Business Week. Yes, it works!

AREN'T ALLOWED IT - When my son, David, was 4 he knew how to solve a problem. Every dirty sock in his clothes hamper housed a stash of crackers and cookies for midnight snacks. That's a pretty impressive level of creativity, because it requires synthesis. So how did we reward that insight? We righteously squashed it.

In our defense, the thought of athlete's lip was a consideration. But in all honesty, we were mostly driven by that parental disease, the desire for control. We determine snack time and content, not the kid. After 13 days in the coal bin on bread and water he stopped stashing the loot.

Now he sits up straight, takes his snacks in the kitchen, and we expect to be very proud of his work as an IRS auditor. However, he does have an unsettling twitch.

Creativity is always a pain in the neck to someone, because there are a lot of earlier coal-bin inhabitants who have risen to positions of power. Consequently, most people's creativity is squashed, and squashed hard, by the powers that be. Organizations - as diverse as the family unit, Proctor and Gamble and the government - all thrive on order and control. Creativity threatens that order on any issue, whether it's snack time or budgetary policy. Consequently, organizations tend to repress creativity, even if they've made a conscious commitment to nurture it. Hopefully, <u>you</u> will break that cycle once you control the coal bin.

The Myths of Creativity
Just for the sake of argument, let's say you've just had a conversion experience. You really want to know creativity, you want to want it and you want to allow it in yourself. Are you home yet? Nope. Those were simply functional barriers: ignorance, desire and freedom. They're relatively easy to deal with. But once you cross those, you've still got a passel of obstacles left which are a lot more insidious to deal with - because they hide among the mythology of life. They're the things that cause those nagging doubts; the kind that lead you to say, "I can't do it because ..... ". And more often than not, the "because" we generate is a bunch of poppycock that we've been sucked into believing. Well it's time to grasp the poppy by its privates and give it a heave. Let's look at, and deal with some of the myths about creativity.

MYTH # 1 - THE MISSING ORGAN - Many people seem to think that creativity is like a mystic organ, say an extra pancreas or enlarged hypothalamus gland, that only a few people possess. In all honesty, they may be correct when it comes to certain forms of invention. However, that is only a fraction of the Great ISM of creativity, and the rest of the model is not dependent on mysticism or revelation. As we saw earlier, if you ever hid food in your bedroom you've got the creative seed to do the other 93% of creativity.

MYTH # 2 - THE NEED FOR GENIUS - Many people also believe that creativity is the result of the <u>amount</u> of intelligence that one possesses. Clinical and field studies, however, fail to support this hypothesis. Verifiable geniuses (as measured by IQ tests and similar instruments) tend to do very well for themselves vocationally, but they usually do so as corporate vice presidents shuffling paper. They haven't made much of a dent in terms of making creative contributions to the world.[2] A solid "C" student with curiosity and determination usually makes a bigger impact on the world. Thomas Edison's teachers thought he was retarded and he was squeezed out of school in the 6th grade. Theodore Geisel, Dr. Seuss, didn't do well in art class. In fact, his professor liked his work best when it was turned upside down. And the Chicago Tribune rejected Walt Disney as an editorial cartoonist – because he lacked a nasty edge.

The key is not <u>how much</u> talent you have, but the <u>type</u> of talent you have, and
your willingness to use it.

Steven Jobs was a back alley hustler with street smarts, not an intellectual. His "genius" was the ability to dream dreams then connive and cajole others into cooperation. Wozniak was his first victim. Once he was under wing, Jobs had something to sell. He waved Wozniak's genius like a flag and convinced lawyers and ad agencies to work for nothing more than the promise of future payments, and Markkula to risk everything he had. Jobs therefore earned his title as the father of Apple, despite the fact that he was neither a technical nor marketing wizard. He was just a jack-of-all-trades, with a whole lot of chutzpa.

MYTH # 3 - THE SOLITARY MAGICIAN - Another myth is that the creative person exists in a vacuum, locked in his garage with God as the only source of inspiration. It makes a great movie script, but usually misses the mark in terms of reality.

Take a look at electricity. The Chinese discovered magnetism while Europeans were still eating with their hands. Frenchmen came up with the first spark maker and discovered alternating current. Ben Franklin generated a good deal of the observations that moved electricity from theory to application. Englishmen invented the first electromagnet, generator and motor. And an academic at Rensselaer Polytechnic Institute was blissfully inventing capacitors, alternators, generators and filters for his own entertainment while Edison was desperately searching for light. So when Thomas Edison sat "alone" in his workshop and "invented" the light bulb, he was hardly alone. Every one of those other folks was crammed into the shadows. They represented the 99% perspiration Edison advocated ... knowing the trail of research. In fact, Edison had made regular visits to Prof. Henry Rowland, that American academic puttering away at Rensselaer.[3]

Creativity exists in a 4th dimension, crossing over normal boundaries of turf, time and vocation.

In fact, it is such a universalistic and international effort that it leads to some pretty odd historical footnotes; such as when the British government guaranteed Ben Franklin safe passage to discuss his electrical theories at the Royal Academy of Science in London at the height of the Revolutionary War. And this despite the fact that Franklin had been Jefferson's ghost writer on the treasonous Declaration of Independence that started the rebellion, and was the publicly acknowledged glue that held the Continental Congress together. The moral here is this:

Creativity thrives on interaction, not seclusion.

It is a vacuum cleaner, and unless you mingle in the dust bowl of humanity, you'll have nothing to suck. So at a minimum, go talk to someone. And use any instrument, gimmick or event to get outside your shell.

MYTH #4 - CREATIVITY AND NOBILITY - Since we tend to envision the creative person locked in his garage with God, we tend to see creativity as the progeny of a sacred union. Sometimes it may be exactly that, but usually not. In fact, there are numerous indications that creativity is the product of someone you'd like to throw in jail.

In 1860 a group of investors paid young Johnnie Rockefeller to make a field investigation of the commercial viability of petroleum. He thought it was a sure fire winner. So he lied through his teeth. He told the investors it was a loser, put every penny of his own funds into petroleum, and aced them out of the market. Then he went on to invent most of the competitive practices that are now illegal. Before he was a philanthropist, John D. Rockefeller was a hustler. But he was also marvelously creative, and the industry still bears his mark in terms of production, distillation and distribution.

In 1790 Samuel Slater stole the trade secrets of mass production in England and sold himself to the highest bidder in America; boldly violating every aspect of international and British patent and copyright law. As a result, he put America on the map as an industrial nation by opening America's first large scale cotton mill, which triggered the eventual collapse of England's textile industry. But Sam redeemed himself. He and his wife were the originators of Sunday School in America. Don't you love it? But wait, it gets better. At the same time he was violating the British, he was the leading advocate of, and lobbyist for, the legislation that established America's own patent and copyright laws.[4] Isn't irony grand?

Creativity isn't very pristine. In fact, it sometimes emanates from the dark side of our personality. That's unsettling if you see business as a quaint tea party. It's intuitively obvious if you recognize it as trench warfare. So with a nod to Freud, the first place you may want to check for ideas is your Id. The second place you'll want to check is the Id of thy neighbor. At its worst, creativity involves outright theft on a grand scale. At its best, it is a form of unconscious plagiarism.

If God accompanies us to the garage, he usually sits there and tells us what our neighbors are doing. So don't be timid about where you look or what you use. Any idea is fair game as a starting point. Even if it's protected, it can inspire a useful offshoot. Apple didn't really "create" anything; but it was brilliant at synthesis and modification. So here's a second moral for this chapter. We've become more concerned about secular righteousness than about how well we are doing our job. Each of us has a bit of the rogue in us, and it's about time we got in touch with it. That's tough to do in a day and age dominated by political correctness and the pressures to obey Big Mom (You remember her. She used to be called Big Brother). To pull it off we've got to confront the whole trap of proper thought and behavior head on.

A. **There is a food chain, and man is on top**. The rest of creation is there to be used for man's benefit, not the other way around. We forget that the One who created them, provided a very specific pecking order, "Let us make man in our own image, and let them have dominion over the fish of the sea, and over the fowl of the air, and over the cattle, and over all the earth, and over every creeping thing that creepeth upon the earth ... subdue it: and have dominion ..." [Genesis 1: 26-28]. We are hamstringing creativity in medicine, food production and other fields by misinterpreting the existence of a face as proof of equality.

B. **True environmentalism means wise exploitation, not protecting earth's virginity**. The instruction manual on planet earth reads, "Be fruitful, and multiply, and replenish the earth ..." [Genesis 1:28]. It does not say "don't touch the goods". But while the arch-conservatives are screaming "don't touch the fetus, even to save a life", the arch-liberals are screaming, "don't touch a tree, even to build a home". In their own way, each is trying to slam the brakes on the progress that comes from creativity. Both sides need to get real.

C. **Conformity usually gets in the way of function**. If someone needs to smoke to work, buy them the cigarettes, get them a fancy ashtray and beg them to make a cloud. And if he can only work at 3:00 am, take him to breakfast at 2:00 am. Imposed conformity is pushing our best talent out the door, and some of them are Samuel Slater's grandchildren. You better watch your fanny.

MYTH # 5 - THE IMPORTANCE OF PRIDE - Many firms don't use the new ideas and technologies that lay close at hand because of something called the "NIH syndrome" (not invented here). This seems to be equal parts pompous disdain, proprietary fastidiousness, and uncertainty about how to exploit new knowledge. Bell & Howell was once a major name in every upscale home. Its 8 mm movie cameras were the bane and blessing of every family gathering and the chronicler of American family history. By 1972 more than 1 million cameras were being sold each year, but by 1981, sales had plummeted by almost 90% and Bell & Howell became a nostalgic name used in <u>Trivial Pursuit</u>. The simplicity of video swept the marketplace while Bell & Howell ignored the new idea. Now the marketplace ignores Bell & Howell.[5] Pride goeth before a fall.

MYTH # 6 - RISK FREE CREATIVITY - That's a cow pie. Creativity, remember, entails stepping out beyond the boundaries; vaulting the wall of rationality and running out into the unknown. That action has loads of stimulus and exhilaration. But there's one thing it doesn't have - safety.

There are few friends, supporters or advocates. Most people feel more comfortable within the wall and will not venture out to join you; especially if you venture very far outside the wall. In fact, if you get out there far enough, some people may take pot shots at you in an attempt to force you back inside the wall. As Everett Dirksen, the old US Senator, used to say, "You know you're out front when everyone else is kicking you in the ass".

There are no benchmarks, because you've left them all behind. That's not too bad if you stay close enough to keep sight of them. But if you go way out in the meadow, you never really know how you're doing or what you should do next. In many respects you become a rank amateur because, anytime you start something new, you're pretty much in the dark. So ...

You might fail. Walt Disney's first gold mine was Waldo the Duck, long before Mickey was even a glimmer in his eye. But a crooked distributor stole the rights to Waldo and Disney went into bankruptcy. Harlan Sanders blew up a whole lot of pressure cookers before he perfected Kentucky Fried Chicken. So what?

There's no place to hide. When you vault the wall and stand in the meadow, you stick out like a sore thumb. If you're lucky you might get the credit for a success. But I can guarantee you one thing - if you're way out in the meadow, you'll certainly get every bit of the blame if you fail. That's a whole lot of risk piled on one person. That's why most people choose not to <u>be</u> creative. Instead, they try to <u>look</u> creative. They run around inside the wall of rationality looking for morsels. Or they plaster themselves against the inside of the wall, hoping that something in the crevices will have been missed by previous searchers. Some even perch atop the wall and occasionally stick a toe over the parapet.

But none of these efforts goes beyond incrementalism. They'll change the shape of the marshmallow in your instant hot chocolate, but they'll never bring out a beverage that makes you smarter, healthier or prettier. That kind of breakthrough comes from someone who's a little "weird" because they're willing to take the risk.

Let's not be too harsh on the incrementalists though. Fancier marshmallows, new colors, minutely improved detergents and all the other products of portfolio management, copy cat practices and product extensions are actually quite useful. They are all good solid innovations and they make life a little easier and more interesting. There's a lot to be said for that. It's just that the world needs more than that if it is to truly prosper. And so does the firm that's looking for a competitive edge. So in the long run, who prospers? The courageous hero or the safe and sure home body? **The hero.** That's why we invented the name.

Courage is the key
that unlocks creativity.

What it feels like to jump
How will I know when I'm creative? What does it feel like? Go ask Amy – my daughter who jumped from skiing to scuba.

- ♦ Creativity is intellectual speed.
- ♦ It's mental wobbling.
- ♦ It's the lack of full control.
- ♦ And it's falling. A lot. And running short of air.

It's the kind of experience that can frighten you unless someone says "This, my friend, is what creativity feels like. And it's ok."

There's a physical rhythm to creativity, as though you're moving to an unheard bit of song. In fact, sometimes you literally move back and forth in your chair, up and down on your toes or with a new bounce to your walk.

And there's a strange optical focus that sets in. Sometimes that means tunnel vision - the only thing you see is the square foot of space in front of your nose - but you see it with incredible visual clarity. At other times is means the faraway gaze. When I composed the first draft of this book, my eyes glazed over and I was distantly aware of absolutely everything in my environment: the bookshelf behind me as well as the words that were appearing on the screen in front of me. It was like a child's absorption in a great adventure book. I was vaguely aware of the words, but mostly I was conjuring the images. Sometimes you go to a different place entirely. Space ceases to exist.

Creativity also feels like the best shrink in the world. Optimism sets in ... even when there's no clear and apparent reason for it. Energy sets in ... even when you've exceeded the recommended daily adult dosage of effort. Passion returns. It swells the breast with meaning and purpose. It intensifies the emotions and wakes up the senses. You literally consume sensations; sometimes savoring them, sometimes simply gulping them, but always on a search for more.

That's what creativity feels like. Once you experience it, you might just flush your Valium and Prozac down the drain.

Don't tell Anyone ...
I'll share a little secret with you that makes all of this a whole lot less scary. It really doesn't take much creativity to do something new enough to have a major impact. That means you don't have to get real weird, you don't have to go way out into the meadow, and you don't have to suffer major traumas, just to get a good idea. In fact, a lot of breakthroughs sit right at the exterior base of the wall, and all you have to do is lower yourself over the edge. Consequently, it's possible to sneak over the wall, grab a brainstorm, and get back home; all before anyone notices.

The hard part's working up the courage to go over the wall at all. After that it's actually pretty easy. In fact, once you get used to being creative it gets pretty easy to go way out in the meadow. Yes, there is a cost to that adventure, but it's manageable. And when you play out there, you have the chance to change the course of history.

A Final Salvo
So here's the final shot for this chapter. Learn to know creativity. Not just what it looks like, but also what it <u>feels</u> like. Once you've done that it'll be like a drug that draws you back to itself. Learn to want creativity. Lip service is cheap, and meaningless. Want it with your soul, not your mouth. Finally, learn to allow creativity in yourself. There will always be coal bins. So invent the flashlight, then show no fear.

End Notes

1. *The opening scenario, and subsequent information on Apple comes from Robert F. Hartley, <u>Marketing Successes</u>, (New York: John Wiley & Sons Inc., 1985) pp. 200-213*

2. *Lewis Terman, father of the American IQ test, discovered this rather enlightening factoid in a 60 year study of 1,528 measurable geniuses. Cited by Leslie Dorman in "Original Spin", <u>Psychology Today</u>, August 1989, pp.47-52*

3. *The historical information on electricity comes from <u>The People's Chronology</u>, James Trager, ed. (New York: Holt, Rinehart and Winston, 1979). In addition to being an entertaining ammunition dump for <u>Trivial Pursuit</u>, it is a fascinating guide to the progression of knowledge. You'd be well served to buy a recent edition.*

4. *<u>The People's Chronology</u>, James Trager, ed. (New York: Holt, Rinehart and Winston, 1979), again. I told you it was good.*

5. *Ann Hughey, "Sales of Home Movie Equipment Falling as Firms Abandon Market, Video Grows", <u>Wall Street Journal</u>, March 17, 1982, p. 25*

5
BRAIN FOOD
(SOME IDEAS YOU'D BETTER MASTER)

You're probably pretty geared up by this point. We've looked at the great ISM of creativity, and you've said to yourself, "I can do that." We've looked at the target of all that creativity, and you've said "Yeh, I can do applications too." And we've wrapped it all in a pep-talk format, so that everything looks doable. So now you're ready to dive in and learn the specifics of doing creativity. But not so fast. You've got one more chapter to read before you get to the goodies. This chapter. And in this one we're going to look at some pretty important points that can be drawn from everything we've discussed to this point. That way, you'll have a solid launch pad for your own career as a creative whiz.

Efficiency vs. Effectiveness

There's a notion floating around out there that creativity can make us more efficient. The fact is the notion's true. It can. But do you really want to be more efficient? Think about it.

- **Efficiency** is the art of coming as close to our goal as possible, for the least possible expense. If we were target shooting, we'd limit ourselves to one bullet, and see how close we came to the bull's eye.

- **Effectiveness**, in contrast, is the art of getting the job done -100% - no matter what it costs. If we were target shooting we'd simply nuke the target area, knowing that the bull's eye, along with everything else, would be obliterated.

Now, which benchmark do you want to use in your own life? If you tell your couch potato son to take out the trash, and he does no more than grunt, how do you feel? You did get some kind of a response from him, and you only had to say something once. That's very efficient. But are you happy? Or will you nag and wail and threaten and generally expend more energy than it would have taken to do the garbage run yourself? Come on, 'fess up. You know you take the route of effectiveness, not efficiency. You'll accomplish the goal (getting <u>him</u> to take out the garbage) come hell or high water. That's effectiveness, and you couldn't comprehend "doing" home any other way. But, do you use the same benchmark when you move from home to office? Let's use an equation from economics to prove a point.

$$P = R - C$$

Profit, as we all know, equals the revenue we pull in, minus the cost we incur (P = R - C). That gives you two options for increasing profit: you can increase revenue (the effectiveness route), or you can cut costs (the efficiency route). So, which do you focus on?

The Creativity Matrix

	INVENT	SYNTH.	MODIFY
IDEA			
PROTO-TYPE			
DEVELOP-MENT			
DELIVERY			
SPINOFFS			The focus of efficiency

NOTE: There are 15 cells in the matrix. 1/15 = 7%

The majority of business people have fallen into the "efficiency trap". They focus on cutting costs. So they lay off a couple thousand employees, they abandon a couple markets, close a few factories, and sell off a hundred retail outlets. And in the short run, they look like heroes. Profits soar.

The problem is that life extends beyond the short run. Next year, there won't be enough employees, factories or retail outlets to make and sell the same number of products. So revenue will sink and they'll have to lay off, close and cutback even more. And so it goes, because one important point got lost in our rush to be efficient

It takes money to make money.

Consequently American industry is in danger of spiraling its way to oblivion, getting more and more efficient at going broke. In addition, a focus on efficiency hamstrings creativity. It directs our attention to spinoffs by modification, the old competitive technique of "Me-too-ism" that we used to deride. That means that many American firms are only using 7% of the creativity available to them (1/15th of the matrix). And they're letting their competitors lay claim to the other 93%. You can't exactly win a war when you say, "Look, I'll keep the slingshot and you guys can have the tanks."

Why do we do that? Why do we wallow in the efficiency trap? Why not be as bold in the office as we are at home? You know the reason as well as I do, it's that nasty little word .... risk.

Risk

In hindsight, the proper use of any idea is always obvious. But foresight is not nearly so clear. The Romans seized the breakthrough of steam's mechanical power, but used it only to run toys. Two thousand years later, Elisha Gray was just as confused. He invented the phone at the same time Bell did. But Gray didn't know what to do with it. He thought it might make a nice intercom around the house, or an entertaining toy. Bell, on the other hand, made a monumental leap in terms of vision. He saw that the phone's real usefulness lay not <u>within a house</u>, but <u>between houses</u>. That seems pretty obvious now, but it was a leap of genius in terms of application and the history of civilization.[1] Then Bell's own company had one of those Elisha Gray moments itself, 90 years later. Bell Labs developed the transistor, the core of our entire computer industry, but didn't know what to do with it. For the first ten years of its existence it was relegated to replacing vacuum tubes in radios and TV's. Old Alexander surely spent the 1960's doing barrel rolls in his grave.

It's a crap shoot. Being creative does not automatically translate into being right. In fact, the majority of creative ideas don't turn out too well.

> The Edsel was clearly the most creative car of its day. It was built for a new target market that was just exploding into view - the suburban junior executive - the yuppie of the 50's. It used a new design, moving from the blue-whale bulk of the 40's to a sleeker line dominated by chrome. Its front end featured a new-fangled vertical grill, and it was loaded with the very latest in automatic functions and controls. And yet the Edsel bombed.

> DuPont invented Corfam, the imitation leather that promised to revolutionize the shoe industry. It came on standard flat sheets that eliminated the wastage of odd sized leather pelts. It eliminated the costly tanning process. It never needed polishing. It was already waterproof, and it didn't pucker or bulge. Yet it was a total failure, because it didn't "breath". Consumers didn't relate to the joy of walking around in a pool of sweat.

The point is that creativity can lead you down the road to failure as well as down the road to success. In fact, creativity probably gives rise to more bad ideas than good ones. We'll cover some of the techniques for weeding out the bad ideas a little later, but for the moment our point is this ... it takes a lot of time and effort, and often a good many false starts, before you get to the great idea that blows open the market.

Creativity is fraught with risk. "Fraught", now there's a great word. It means filled to a point of abundance. And that pretty much sums up creative risk. It is abundant. That's why most folks hide inside the old wall. As Harry Truman said, "If you can't take the heat, stay out of the kitchen." But you're made of asbestos, so don't worry. We know this, because you're still reading. So you can take the heat. Anyway, a little later in the book we'll look at some ways to lower the temperature of risk.

Time
Creativity ain't quick.
- Crunk the caveman, or whatever his name was, discovered fire in 8,508 B.C. (I think it was on a Thursday)
- Mabel and Crunk's dance of **general** ideas actually extended over the next 10,000 years,
- until da Vinci had the full blown **specific** idea for a steam engine in 1492.
- Then 273 years passed until James Watt made the first prototype in 1765. Think about that. Two hundred and seventy three years. And you get discouraged if your idea isn't acted on within a month?
- Then it was another 20 years before the first steam engine was put into commercial practice.
- Finally, new products appeared each day for the next 20 years and mankind exploded into the steam age.

There is often a considerable time lag between the first breakthrough on an idea and its successful application. In fact, "time-lag" is sometimes an understatement. Fortunately, the time frame is usually shorter than that of the steam engine's appearance. But, from start to finish, all ideas take time. The supermarket and the television both took about 30 years to become functional successes. The microwave took 20. Music videos took about 15.

We have yet to stumble on an overnight success, except perhaps, for fads such as the hula hoop and pet rock. But they're not around anymore. And before you throw Steven Jobs' overnight success at Apple in my face as an exception to that rule, let me point something out. It took about 10,000 years for cavemen to figure out the difference between the number 1 and the number 2. Several thousand more years passed before the Chinese invented the first calculator - called the abacus. And that was before the time of written history. So it was only about 17,000 more years until Apple came out with the PC. Some overnight sensation, huh?

Another thing to notice, and this is a hopeful sign, is that the time frames compress as we move from idea to delivery. And it shrinks at a geometric rate. It took 10,000 years to go from the first general idea to the specific idea for the steam engine. But it took only 273 years to move from there to a prototype, and only 20 years to go from there to the first delivered working model. After that, new spinoffs appeared almost daily. That is an amazing performance improvement, and it occurs because of the increasing number of people who vault the old wall and come to join us. They each bring their own talents and skills, creating the critical mass of knowledge required to move ahead quicker and quicker. But, it's still a slow process isn't it?

Lasting creativity takes time. And that translates into costs, which is why an efficiency mindset is the enemy of any meaningful creativity. It hates cost.

You can get a little antsy waiting 2,000 years or 20, or even 2. You can also get discouraged, when faced with a string of failures. Yet if you don't have the patience it takes to nurture creativity, you'll never reap the rewards. Just watch out for the trap. Patience can easily slip into passivity. We can sit patiently starring at a wall and say "I can't scale it". Or we can patiently dig little toe holds and inch our way to the top, like the little engine that could. Don't confuse the two. In fact, let me put this point in big print, because it's one of the major keys to this book.

!

PATIENCE IS <u>NOT</u> A VIRTUE. PATIENCE IS A <u>TOOL</u>.

!

The biggest enemy you face is your own short term mentality. So burn your quarterly reports and shoot their authors. If you can't think beyond the next three months you'll never amount to a hill of beans. Creativity is a long haul proposition.

Necessity Is A Mother
If nothing else, you will have noticed by this time that creativity requires a lot of physical and psychic energy. And humans are, by nature, very efficient. If something doesn't need doing, we don't waste the effort on it. It's one of the ways we conserve our energy and mental capacity, to

guard against burn out. Consequently, creativity, like any other task, usually sits in the wings until necessity commands its appearance. World War I speeded up the development of the airplane by a good two decades. World War II did the same to nuclear energy. The bottom line is that there have to be compelling reasons before people invest the time and effort to be creative. That's why it usually doesn't kick in until people have their backs against a wall. "Desperation is a good motive" said David Luther, the head of quality control at Corning. "Customers came to us and said if we didn't change, they'd go somewhere else."[2] Since that time Corning has been tremendously motivated and has worked itself back into the position where it is once again widely praised for its creativity.[3] "Necessity", as they say, "is the mother of invention". .... It's also the concubine of synthesis and modification.

The Competitive Edge

Two newlyweds encountered a hungry bear in the forest. The woman immediately bent down and tightened her shoelaces. The husband asked incredulously, "You don't think you're going to outrun that bear, do you?"

The wife smiled sweetly and said "I don't have to outrun the bear, darling. I just have to outrun you."

Your ideas don't have to unlock the secrets of the universe; they just have to be better than your competitors'. That's the key here, folks. It's why creativity is worthwhile. You can get massive returns from a surprisingly small creation. That should be a comfort since most of us don't sit in the garage at God's right hand.

The competition's not that tough to beat, if you put your mind to the task. Don't take my word for it. Just take a look at the numbers. When Booz, Allen & Hamilton did a five year study on new product introductions, they found that God wasn't anywhere near most people's garage.
- ◆ Only 10% of the products qualified as new products
- ◆ 26% were simply improved revisions
- ◆ 26% were product line extensions, i.e. bringing out mittens to complement an existing line of gloves
- ◆ 20% were primarily imitations of competitor's products
- ◆ 11% were cheaper versions of existing products, and
- ◆ 7% were just an introduction of an existing product to a new market (repositioning).[4]

That's pretty depressing if you're looking at this from a societal standpoint. But if you're in business yourself, and looking for a competitive edge, you ought to be bouncing off the walls in glee. Your competitors are forfeiting a competitive edge to you any time you show up with a product, service or idea that's really new. The vast bulk of products, services and marketing efforts are simply fine tuning of what's safe and proven. They don't even qualify as a modified spinoff, which is the lowest form of creativity. That means that if you pushed yourself a bit you could clean up. Even a good solid modification would put you in a niche all by yourself.

Some Partially Useful Clichés

<u>Education is the route to success</u> - Education is touted as the panacea of society and the meal ticket for individuals. But if you take a look at the creative notables, they were often people with little or no formal education. The person who mastered fire didn't have a PhD. In fact, education often stands in the way of ideas and even prototypes, because it emphasizes socialization, not curiosity, revelation or functional serendipity. Paul MacCready, our modern day Edison, (the one who's invented the first practical electric car and man-powered airplane) relies on the "... innocence of wonder. He approaches problems and learning about new things in the same way, without strongly held, preconceived notions."[5] Neither of these traits is encouraged in school. And who knows? That may be appropriate, you simply can't teach inventive ability. The best you can do is teach synthesis and modification.

But let's not pooh-pooh education and training. They are absolutely crucial when we turn our attention to the laborious and systematic work of development and delivery. At that point socialization and technical skills are necessary conditions for success.

Teamwork is the key to success - Societies praise it, schools teach it and organizations demand it. But to what purpose? Ideas are the province of the individual. Think about that for a moment. When you cut to the core, it is impossible for two people to simultaneously have the same original idea. The best they can do is toss their own individual contributions into a pot and hammer out a hybrid. Aha! That's the excuse for groups. The hybrid is often an improvement over the original idea. The problem is that teamwork can get so claustrophobic that the individuals don't have the breathing space to originate the initial ideas. So the group ends up hammering on nothing. We draw from this that teamwork is useful, not sacred.

Research will show us the answers - There's a lot to be said for the precision of the scientific approach.

- It lets us work out the theories, details and feasibility before we incur the expense of building a prototype or hauling a product to market.
- It thoroughly tests ideas before we waste money on lousy products, advertising campaigns or manufacturing procedures.
- It's based on precedent, so our grand leaps are not so grand that we'll get in trouble.
- It injects a high level of efficiency into our efforts on development, delivery and spinoffs.

And it gives us loads of numbers. Oh Lord how we love those numbers. They give us the ammo to defend our ideas to others. And they also give us a scapegoat when things go wrong. We can always say, "Gee, boss, you saw the numbers. They looked good." But research isn't much good for the really interesting ideas, which usually come from serendipity (fortunate accidents).

Research didn't lead to the discovery of fire, luck did. And research didn't lead to Einstein's Theory of Relativity either. That was the product of revelation, pure and simple. By his own admission, Albert got the inspiration first then worked backward to recreate a stream of mathematical logic that would help his colleagues accept the theory.

Even academic historians are starting to acknowledge that the great theories, and monumental product breakthroughs, were the result of inspiration or revelation, not research. In short, the cart was pulling the horse.

The upshot of all this is that there seems to be a societal bias toward the bottom of the Creativity Matrix. Education, teamwork and research combine to build a culture and critical mass of skills that focus directly on the mechanics of doing better work in development, delivery and spinoffs. But - and this is a very big but - education, teamwork and research also serve as a brake on the kind of individual creativity that leads to basic ideas and prototypes.

So we face a societal problem. Unless we put an equal emphasis on the startup points of ideas and prototypes, development and delivery are like superhighways with nowhere to go. As Akio Morita, America's foremost Japanese critic said, "America is by no means lacking in [basic] technology. But it does lack the creativity [the ideas and vision] to apply new technologies commercially. This, I believe, is America's biggest problem. On the other hand, it is Japan's strongest point."[6] I just tossed that quote in to irritate and motivate you a little more. I also tossed it in to move us to our next topic ... culture.

The Creativity Matrix

	INVENT	SYNTH.	MODIFY
IDEA			
PROTOTYPE			
DEVELOPMENT		The focus of Education Teamwork & Research	
DELIVERY			
SPINOFFS			The focus of efficiency

Culture and Creativity

As it turns out, Morita was absolutely right ... but for the wrong reason. He thought the solution was a <u>managerial</u> one, simply shifting the focus of corporate attention. What he didn't seem to realize was that the problem is <u>cultural</u>, not managerial. And using managerial tools to address a cultural issue makes as much sense as using a rolling pin to build a house. At some point, management needs to wake up to the fact that sometimes you have to adjust to culture, rather than ignore it. This is a weighty, as well as crucial, issue ... so let's get a little historical perspective on the matter.

Up until 1945, America stayed in the forefront of industrial creativity by focusing on the invention of ideas and prototypes. Then World War II left our major competitors bombed into submission and we were the only major industrial power still intact. So we took a break, and our creativity retreated into a very narrow pocket of spinoffs via modification. Mostly, we just kept upgrading the tried and proven ideas of the past. It was safe, it showed immediate returns, and it was expedient. In short, it was efficient. It popularized television, which was a product of the 1930's. It brought us color TV, which was nice, but nothing really new. The same was true of power steering, the dishwasher, the touch-tone phone and a host of similar products. America was successful, comfortable and very complacent.

But within 25 years the Germans and Japanese had rebuilt their impressive physical plants and by 1970 they were back in business, with a physical plant that was two generations newer than ours, driven by new fangled management ideas that we had laughed out of the U.S. workplace. Ideas like quality control, cost effectiveness, communal work groups, and decision modes. They started beating us at our own game, with modifications that were quicker, better and cheaper.

We counter attacked ... with advertising. Oh, it was good, clever, hard hitting, and pervasive. But it did absolutely nothing to reverse America's fortunes because it had absolutely nothing to do with making better products.

Advertising, it turns out, is most effective when there's really nothing but image that differentiates products. It's not much good, however, when the products are clearly so different. We kept at it, anyway, for another ten years.

Finally, when the Koreans became a world class player, we heard our wake up call. Germany and Japan, after all, were simply reclaiming their rightful places in the industrial club. But Korea had never even visited the club in the first place. It was a third world nation that was effectively in the Stone Age by the end of the Korean War. So when they started taking our customers in steel, ship building and automobiles, we finally decided it was time to get serious.

We discovered that all three competitors were wonderful synthesizers and modifiers, who worked wonders when it came to development, delivery and spinoffs. They swept the world like vacuum cleaners, ingesting the inventions from other lands and coming out a year later with an upgraded version that outperformed the original.

So we threw our entire creative genius into beating the enemy where he stood. Business became the biggest undergraduate major. MBA programs became the necessary credential for success, as they turned themselves into rigorous boot camps for the systematic analysis and management that development work requires. Every major firm restructured. Research and development budgets blossomed; and American industry was filled with management systems, systematic programs, programming systems and systematic structured management programs ad nauseam. By 1985 we had systems, programs and management efforts coming out the ears. But the American economy continued to falter despite it all. Why? Because the great thinkers who did all this retooling forgot the two truisms that every 2nd lieutenant knows.

1. Never let the enemy determine where the battle will be fought. They always pick the location that benefits them, not you.
2. Never, repeat never, copy the enemy's tactics. They can do them better than you, and they also know the best defense against those tactics.

We were fighting a losing battle because we were on the battlefield chosen by the enemy (development), and were trying to copy their tactics (modification). The Czar used to shoot generals who were that dumb.

America had fallen into a cultural trap. We decided to compete in an arena where the foreigners have a decided cultural advantage. Japan, Korea and Germany are all rigidly hierarchical, technocratic and communal cultures. That's a mouthful which translates into this:
- They like to take orders.
- They like highly structured, lock-step procedures.
- They like traditions, policies and precision; and
- They love working together and sharing the credit.

In short, they're naturals at development work before they even finish 2nd grade. Incremental, communal efforts are part and parcel of their cultures.

American culture, however, breeds individualistic swashbucklers: the John D. Rockefellers, Thomas Edisons, Lee Iacoccas, and Andrew Carnegies of the world. The kind of folks who see the big picture, think that precision is measured by "close enough", and take bold risks. And that's just as well, since Americans have short attention spans. We get bored with details, we're too self-absorbed to have a cooperative communal mentality, and we are lousy at obedience. Americans are a cantankerous lot. So, if there's one section of the Creativity Matrix that we're culturally least suited for it's - you guessed it - modification as it applies to development, delivery and spinoff work. It brings out the worst in us. We get complacent, sloppy and lazy. And yet, that is precisely the section of the matrix that we were trying to master. Talk about self-imposed defeat. It makes about as much sense as teaching a pig to sing. You never get a melody. You just wear out the farmer and irritate the pig.

> Instead of learning to be someone else, Americans might be better served by relearning how to be American.

Historically speaking, this would entail returning to invention as it pertains to ideas and prototypes. It's a precarious strategy, because it means you have to constantly stay one step ahead of the competition. But there's a lot to be said for focusing on your strengths. Just don't go off half-cocked. This doesn't mean that Americans should ignore development. We should just realize that, for us, development is a defensive rather than offensive weapon. Our competitive edge will occur elsewhere.

Can Americanized Creativity Work?

Corning broke itself into over 3,000 teams of no more than 15 people, in an effort to re-approach the good old days of the independent inventor. The results? It's production of successful new products soared and its profits rose by 250% between 1982 and 1990.[7]

Kodak turned management of one film plant over to its blue collar workers, getting the systematic MBA types out of the way so that the creative ideas and practices of Joe six-pack could have the freedom to rise to the surface. The result? One Kodak plant went from operating at $1 million over budget to running $1.5 million under budget. And that $2.5 million turnaround was actually much larger when you add in the money not spent on "experts".[8] The strategy worked so well that General Motors borrowed the idea when it opened its Saturn plant.

Nowadays, we encounter Kodak and Saturn while playing Trivial Pursuit™, if at all. Their names are no longer part of our daily experience, because ... well, because the world changed, and they didn't. Doing something creative, no matter how big, doesn't set you up for a life time of fame and fortune; because there is always some new kid with a newer creative idea that can squeeze you right out of the market (as happened to Saturn) or simply evaporate your entire industry (as digital technology did to the film industry).

But back to our central point - 3M stimulates its employees to act like individuals rather than employees by encouraging them to spend up to 15% of their time on non-job related activities, or on "skunk works" which are simply any valid ideas the employee wishes to pursue. One third of 3M's annual revenue now comes from products developed during the past 5 years, and 70% of its annual $12 billion in sales comes from ideas originated by workers near the bottom of the organization, not near the top.

Look at what these successes entailed:
1. a return to relying on individuals, not systems;
2. decentralization to get away from group mentality and systematic straightjackets;
3. the freedom to invent and synthesize; and
4. the safety to pursue new ideas and prototypes.

So can Americanized creativity work? You can bet your wallet on it, because it meshes with the American culture instead of fighting against it.

Where Do We Go From Here?
We go to boot camp. From here on out this book is a manual, a "how-to" cookbook. We'll start with techniques for enhancing your own personal creativity and then take a look at the structure and process involved. And by the time you finish, you'll have a trunk full of tools, the know-how to use them, and the confidence to try. Fasten your seat belt. It's time to move.

End Notes

1. Eugene Linden, "Dashed Hopes and Bogus Fears", *Time*, June 11, 1990, p. 58

2. Jay Cocks, "Let's Get Crazy", *Time*, June 11, 1990, p. 40

3. Keith Hammonds, "Corning's Class Act", *Business Week*, May 13, 1991, pp. 68-76

4. *New Products Management for the 1980's*, (New York: Booz, Allen & Hamilton, 1982)

5. Leon Jaroff, "He Gives Wings to Dreams", *Time*, June 11, 1990, p. 52

6. Akio Morita and Shintaro Ishihara, *The Japan That Can Say No*, Kobunsha Publishers, Tokyo, 1989, and "A Japanese View: Why America Has Fallen Behind", *Fortune*, September 25, 1989, p. 52

7. Eugene Linden, "Dashed Hopes and Bogus Fears", *Time*, June 11, 1990

8. Leon Jaroff, "He Gives Wings to Dreams", *Time*, June 11, 1990

6
OPEN THE DOOR
(THE ART OF CREATIVE THINKING)

Your doorbell just rang. When you peek through the peep hole you'll think you see a door-to-door salesman. But don't be fooled. It's really a disguise. What you really see is the first concrete step in our nuts and bolts techniques for getting creative.

Linear Thinking

Linear thinking dominates most of our activities, even for something as simple as answering the door. It is an absolutely rational and logical thought process that strings together a host of if-then propositions, so that we move from point A (the stimulus) to point B (our action) in a straight line, with no wasted thought or effort – like the example below. Now think about that for a second.

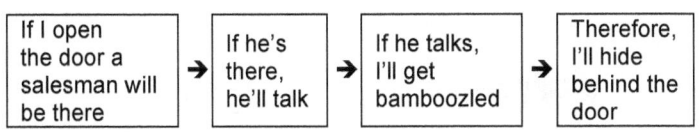

Oh, that's clever. You're probably the first homeowner who's ever pulled that one: the old "I'm a prisoner in my own home" routine. Ask yourself this: wouldn't it be just a tad bit more fun to use a little creativity and live the following scenario?

Explosive Thinking

If I open the door, a salesman will be outside

His job is to sell me something I don't want	Opening the door obligates me to listen	I wonder why he entered sales	I bet he gets lots of hostility	He's probably desperate for a sale
Therefore, he'll try to bamboozle me	I wonder if knocking puts an obligation on him	I wonder if he's any good	A warm response would disarm him	desperation would make me very tired
I get tired of being bamboozled	I'll bet he has an obligation to listen too	If so, he wouldn't be a door to door salesman	What should I do when he's disarmed	Fatigue needs a place to sit
I could ignore the door	I've got lots of things I'd like to say to a salesman	If not, he's poor and has to buy 2nd hand stuff	Hmmm, it would be nice to turn the tables	If he had a drink, he'd want to sit down
But it would be nice to turn the tables	I'd like to try out-talking a salesman	I'd like to unload that old sofa	Let's dump the old sofa on him	That old sofa'd feel pretty good

Sell him the Sofa!

Welcome to the World of Explosive Thinking

Admit it. Unloading the sofa was a lot more satisfying than hiding behind your door, wasn't it? And in the process, you experienced your first concrete tool for getting creative. It's called explosive thinking, and it differs from linear thinking in several interesting ways.

- ◆ Linear thinking deals with one thought at a time. Explosive thinking entertains a room full of the little buggers simultaneously.
- ◆ Linear thinking is absolutely focused, like a rifle. Explosive thinking is more like a shotgun, producing a multitude of seemingly unrelated thoughts.
- ◆ As a result, linear thinking rarely makes a mistake, because it is the epitome of step-by-step logic.
- ◆ Explosive thinking, on the other hand, <u>can</u> make mistakes, because its complexity defies precise control.

Consequently, linear thinking has the look and feel of two-fisted rationality. Explosive thinking looks down right flaky. And therein lies the obstacle for many would-be creative folks. No one wants to be a fool. But stop a minute and notice something. Explosive thinking is actually every bit as rational as linear thinking. Each element of the explosion is merely a logical branching of the original train of thought.

The Big "So what?"

Those additional branches never occur to the linear thinker. He's so busy moving efficiently from point A to point B that he misses anything that's not directly on "the line". But explosive thinking misses nothing. The universe is its path from A to B.

As a result, <u>linear thinking</u> often goes on automatic pilot and repeats an entire set of responses based on nothing more than an initial external stimulus. This makes us very efficient, but in the process it traps us in a very narrow range of ideas and applications. We simply miss a lot of obvious chances to be creative. In short, everything a linear thinker experiences is driven by the external stimulus, the doorbell.

Meanwhile the <u>explosive thinker</u> is reacting not only to the doorbell, but also to all the thoughts and ideas that were triggered by hearing the doorbell. So the explosive thinker gets twice as many ideas because he is sucking stimulus from twice as many sources - internal as well as external. These multiple streams of thought will trigger brainstorms that the linear thinker will never see.

Do you remember when I told you that the creativity was already inside you, and all you had to do was relax enough to let it out? <u>This</u> is what I meant.

You have this amazing warehouse of priceless intuition in there. All you have to do is relax enough to let the explosion occur. This is the crux of creativity.

These explosions - both large and small - are the things that carry us beyond the normal boundaries of life. They change our roles, and our goals. And they change the behavior that goes with both.

Our little door-to-door scenario is a good example. Consumers usually go on automatic pilot and buy into the role of passive defender: ignoring the door, closing the door, or fending off aggression. The explosive approach can carry you beyond those normal boundaries, and transform you into the aggressive seducer, which is a whole lot more fun and profitable.

The Need for Linear Thinking

I just made linear thinkers look like passive little schmucks. So why am I re-introducing linear thought as a useful technique? Because it's a necessity. Explosive thinking may be the source of the glorious ideas, but linear thinking is the technique that carries us to useful applications. That may be the strongest message to come from the Apple example. Jobs, Markkula and Wozniak combined explosive and linear thought across the board. Every problem brought an explosion of off the wall ideas, followed by the kind of nuts and bolts linear logic that brought them to fruition. Obviously, we're best served by an approach that combines the two.

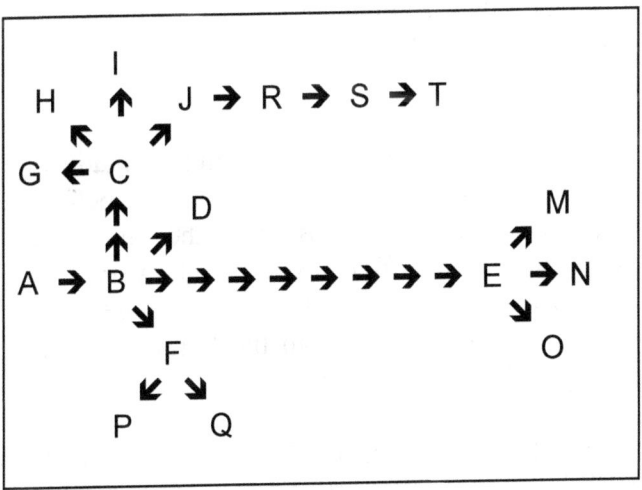

There is, therefore, no intention to diminish the importance of the linear aspect. It's just that there is little reason to devote time to it since we've been trained in the linear approach all our lives. We'll simply concentrate on the explosive side, because it is the avenue that's been ignored.

Just Plain Thinking

The Music Man rolled into River City, full of bamboozle, snake oil and charm. His goal was to bilk the country rubes out of their life savings; and he did this by convincing them to pay in advance for band uniforms and instruments that would never arrive. But the coup de grace, which gave him endless satisfaction, was the additional scam of having them pay for music lessons, free from contact with any musical instrument. The kids simply sat empty handed in an auditorium, while the Music Man had them "think" the music over and over again.

If you saw the movie, you know the outcome. The rubes nailed him. They kept him a virtual prisoner until instruments actually arrived. They heated up the tar and feathers. Then they commanded the kids to "play", just to prove the Music Man's chicanery before riding him out of town on a rail.

But wonder of wonders, the kids actually made music - without ever having touched an instrument before. The Music Man was as flabbergasted as the town folks, but recovered his wits sufficiently to lead everyone in the rousing show-stopper, "76 Trombones", before fading into the sunset with the girl (Marian the librarian), and a new found respect for human potential.

When you stop to think of it, things in the real world aren't much different. We have oriental instructors teaching near infants to play virtuoso violin in much the same fashion. Sports psychologists earn mega-bucks by having basketball stars stand at the foul line and repeatedly visualize sinking free throws, without even touching the ball. And art teachers have been improving the performance of students for years by telling them graphic stories which the students must visualize rather than draw.

These phenomena border on the fantastic and have, therefore, attracted a fair amount of academic research. The findings are that creativity - and performance - are based primarily on mindset, not physical technique. It has more to do with the general way in which we envision the world, and ourselves, than with the specific things we do.

That's why the first five chapters of this book were a direct assault on your brain. I want you to think that you're creative, or at least that you could be. Because once you get to that point, most of the battle is won. The rest has to do with thinking about the specific problem or opportunity you face. All you need for that is an anchor and a few techniques.

An Anchor for Your Thoughts
Let's take stock. We know about the Great ISM. We know that necessity in the mother of invention (and synthesis and modification as well). We know that the application process travels through ideas, prototypes, development, delivery and spinoffs. And now we know about explosive thinking, linear thinking and just plain thinking. But frankly, without some kind of a functional anchor, all this marvelous knowledge just spins around in never-never land. What we need is an anchor. But how do we get one?

We invent it. Come on. You should know that by now. In fact, old Igor Ansoff (honest, that's not a stage name) invented just such an anchor back in 1957, and it's been used by executives, mental health counselors and new product designers ever since.[1] I call it the Opportunity Model, and as you can see, it's just a combination of the tools we might use, and the situations in which we might use them. Very pretty, Igor. But how does it work? Before we answer that one, we have to establish something very important:

	EXISTING SITUATION	NEW SITUATION
EXISTING TOOLS	IMPROVE	PIONEER
NEW TOOLS	REDESIGN	DIVERSIFY

The Opportunity Model is a location, not a technique. You can use synthesis to improve, pioneer, redesign and/or diversify. The same is true of all the other techniques. The only thing the Opportunity Model does is trigger your imagination and anchor your thoughts. Each of the concepts and techniques we've covered so far (and those we will soon discover) fit within the Opportunity Model. In fact, each block of the model can hold all of the concepts and techniques in this book, simultaneously.

SO, HOW DO YOU USE IT? You stare at this matrix until you get a little bleary-eyed, then ask yourself:

1. Whether you want to deal with an existing situation (which could include specific people, problems or opportunities) or a new and different situation; and also ask yourself

2. Whether you want to use your existing tools (which could include the products you sell, the talents you possess or the approaches you've mastered) or a new tool.

	EXISTING SITUATION	*NEW SITUATION*
EXISTING TOOLS	**IMPROVE** ▶ Wall Vaulting ▶ The Great ISM ▶ Applications ▶ Effectiveness ▶ Patience ▶ Explosive Thinking ▶ Linear Thinking ▶ Other Techniques	**PIONEER** ▶ Wall Vaulting ▶ The Great ISM ▶ Applications ▶ Effectiveness ▶ Patience ▶ Explosive Thinking ▶ Linear Thinking ▶ Other Techniques
NEW TOOLS	**REDESIGN** ▶ Wall Vaulting ▶ The Great ISM ▶ Applications ▶ Effectiveness ▶ Patience ▶ Explosive Thinking ▶ Linear Thinking ▶ Other Techniques	**DIVERSIFY** ▶ Wall Vaulting ▶ The Great ISM ▶ Applications ▶ Effectiveness ▶ Patience ▶ Explosive Thinking ▶ Linear Thinking ▶ Other Techniques

Your answers to these questions will give rise to the four optional directions to travel, all of which revolve around the ideas and applications we discussed earlier.

THE IMPROVE OPTION (Existing situations and tools) Not too many years ago, chicken was just chicken. You couldn't tell one from the other. It was a commodity. Then Frank Purdue stepped on the scene and dinner has never been the same. First, he worked on quality, so that his birds would be worth your attention. They had a little more meat.

	EXISTING SITUATION	NEW SITUATION
EXISTING TOOLS	**IMPROVE** **Frank Purdue & his magic chicks**	PIONEER
NEW TOOLS	REDESIGN	DIVERSIFY

Next, he fed the chicken in a way that gave it a pleasing golden color when it was naked and wrapped in cellophane - kind of like a poultry suntan.

And finally, Frank went on the tube for an extensive advertising campaign, which turned out to be a master stroke. I mean, Frank Purdue looked like a chicken. His bald head, prominent nose and receding chin combined with his high-pitched nasal twang to yield the definite impression of a rooster in heat. I don't know about you, but if I want the best chicken, I'm gonna buy from the guy that obviously knows best ... the head rooster.

Purdue's incredible wealth lets us know that sometimes creativity doesn't have to leave our own backyard. We stay in the same situation (he still sold to housewives) and use the same tools (he still sold chicken). We just find new and creative ways to combine the two.

THE PIONEER OPTION (New situation, existing tools)
This option leads you to consider how to get more mileage out of the same tool by applying it to new people, problems or opportunities. Jockey had spent years positioning their

underwear as a very macho garment for men. Then they woke up and realized men were actually a lousy market; at least compared to women.

	EXISTING SITUATION	NEW SITUATION
EXISTING TOOLS	IMPROVE Frank Purdue & his magic chicks	**PIONEER** **Jockey's hugging new curves**
NEW TOOLS	REDESIGN	DIVERSIFY

Women wear underpants too, and in incredible abundance. The average guy has nine pair of underwear in his drawer. The average female stockpiles around 25. And she replaces them every 9 months, as soon as one gets faded or pops a stitch. Middle aged men, however, still proudly wear the same lucky pair they had in high school and look at the holes as useful points of ventilation.

So what do you do? After an extensive development effort, which is what executives call studying beautiful young models in their underwear, Jockey used the same old product (underpants) to garner a new market (women). They eliminated the fly, skimped on the material used, and sold the modified version as soft cuddly panties, at an inflated price. Ah, the height of femininity. Who said business couldn't be fun?

THE REDESIGN OPTION-(Same situation, new tools)
Let's say you're a miller who'd like to sell more flour to the average American household. But you notice that the demand for flour is actually dropping. Bummer. Instead of

baking, families are buying more cookies from Nabisco and you figure that's because baking takes too much time. So you haul out the Opportunity Model to see what you can do.

	EXISTING SITUATION	NEW SITUATION
EXISTING TOOLS	IMPROVE Frank Purdue & his magic chicks	PIONEER Jockey's hugging new curves
NEW TOOLS	**REDESIGN** **Bisquick, the** **egg-less wonder**	DIVERSIFY

In a brainstorm born of desperation you augment your flour with salt, soda, powdered eggs and everything else that could speed up the baking process. All customers have to do is spit in it and its ready to go in the oven. Now call the product Bisquick and voila! Sales take off like a rocket. Bisquick was a new tool (via modification) used to address the same old situation (the American kitchen).

THE DIVERSIFY OPTION - (New Situation and tool)
Did you ever notice that the person waiting on you in McDonalds is as likely to be an old geezer as a teenager? How did that happen?

McDonald's used to employ only kids. And to recruit those kids they advertised flexible hours, team spirit, good preparation for running General Motors, and fun, fun, fun. Using teenagers kept salaries down and emphasized McDonalds' image as young and all American. It also drove the store managers nuts.

	EXISTING SITUATION	NEW SITUATION
EXISTING TOOLS	IMPROVE Frank Purdue & his magic chicks	PIONEER Jockey's hugging new curves
NEW TOOLS	REDESIGN Bisquick, the egg-less wonder	**DIVERSIFY** **The aging of McDonalds**

Have you ever tried to schedule the help when every single one of them has a prom on the same night? Have you ever tried to engender team spirit when the employees happen to attend the town's arch rivals? And have you ever tried to get a little corporate discipline in a bunch of kids who actually believe that the job should be fun, fun, fun? Not surprisingly, McDonalds soured on its idea of a youthful staff and decided to go after an entirely new employee pool - retirees - they'd also work for minimum wage, but they had good work habits, didn't date and had no illusions about becoming the corporate vice president. However, to attract this new crowd, McDonalds had to use an entirely different set of tools.

- ♦ Instead of fun, they sold responsibility - somebody needed you.
- ♦ Instead of team spirit, they sold safety monitoring – if you didn't show up for work someone would come looking for you.
- ♦ And instead of selling a future career at GM, they sold the simple notion of having something to do - they fought the bone crushing boredom of widowhood.

The resulting productivity was so good that McDonalds has been able to successfully withstand very aggressive price wars from Taco Bell, Burger King and other contenders.

Let's Review

Synthesis can occur in any of the four blocks of the Opportunity model. <u>You</u> decide which one. The same is true of modification, spinoffs, general and specific ideas - the works. <u>You</u> decide. Not the model. Not your mother. You. This model is simply a road map, showing the locations where creativity can occur. And to tell you the truth, one of the reasons this model has been around for 40 years is because it's a fine map. Thanks, Igor.

When Ideas go Wrong

"Wow!" you think. "This opportunity model is magic. All I've got to do is ponder it a bit, and marvelous ideas are going to flood my brain." Well ... yes and no. You will get ideas. But they won't all be marvelous.

Take the American Dairy Council for instance. They faced a real problem. As soon as kids get old enough to say "no" to Mom without getting decked, they stop drinking milk. You can survive that problem during a baby boom, because there's a constant supply of new drinkers coming down the pike. But as soon as the birth rate drops, your cows are only good for hamburger.

The obvious solution was classic pioneering. Take the same old tool (milk) into a new situation by selling it to a new market; the ultimate consumer - teenagers. Great idea. But how? I know! Teenagers are dating and hanging around with friends. Social acceptance is the end-all and be-all of their lives. All we have to do is change the image of milk. It's not a nutrition drink anymore. No way. Milk, my friend, had just become an incredibly cool social drink. And the American Dairy Council embarked on a multi-million dollar ad campaign that said just that. It showed groups of fun loving teenagers begging for milk at the pizza parlor; young lovers smooching over a romantic glass of milk with two straws; and high school jocks guzzling cool refreshing milk before during and after a heated game on the old sandlot. Milk was in. It was cool. It was young and hip. And it was ridiculous.

- ◆ Have you ever kissed someone with milk-breath? Which did you like best; the odor, or the adhesive gumminess on the surface of their tongue?
- ◆ Have you ever taken a drink of milk in the midst of running your butt off on the playing field? It's a great way to make instant yogurt.
- ◆ To its credit, milk does work ok with pizza, but that got lost in the midst of the absurdity of the rest of the campaign.

The death knell for the campaign was aired on successive editions of the original <u>Saturday Night Live</u> broadcast, as Chevy Chase graphically acted out the milk-breath and instant yogurt problems before a national TV audience. Within 2 weeks the advertising campaign was canceled, and the American Dairy Council went silent for 10 years, until it had another bright idea. This time around they decided to do the impossible by going back to the basics of convincing teenagers and young adults to drink their milk ... because it was good for them. But this time the council tapped into a motivator that worked. Look at their ads.

> A flat-chested 12 year old, ignored by the guys, guzzles her milk and in the course of 30 seconds transforms into a 36-C 18 year old that makes strong men weak.

> A scrawny 12 year old boy is picked on by every locker room bully. He nurses a tall cool milk and transforms into an 18 year old Arnold Schwarzenegger that gets

the proper respect, nay terror and obeisance, from those same bullies.

The tag line says it all, "Milk. It does a body good." But forget what it <u>says</u>. What it <u>means</u> is ...
- ◆ "Milk. It's breast fertilizer", and/or
- ◆ "Milk. It buys a little respect."

In short, the message is ... "Milk. It gives you a bod to die for". Not surprisingly, milk consumption by teens spiked.

Reality Check Time

Notice something. The Opportunity Model, applied to the same tool (milk) and the same situation (teenagers), provided two diametrically opposed results. One was a public embarrassment and the other was a sure fire winner. We'd all feel a lot better if the model gave us a winner every time. But instead, it just stimulates ideas, good as well as bad. Why is that?

Well, it's not the model's fault. So don't write any angry letters to old Igor Ansoff. The problem is the user. In its initial effort, The American Dairy Council started well, then went on automatic pilot and forgot to think. You see, the goodness and badness of any idea depends on who you're addressing, and where they're located relative to that old nemesis - the wall.

The Dairy Council performed a marvelous initial leap, vaulted the old nutrition wall and built a new sociability wall out in the meadow. They just forgot that the teenagers of the world were still hanging around behind their own wall afraid to try anything that might make them unpopular and uncool. And believe me, odor is one of the chief terrors inside that wall.

One of my daughters (who shall remain nameless, for my safety), used to be a perfectly normal human being. She loved to climb trees, play ball with the guys, sweat like a pig and scratch herself in public. Then puberty hit and she got weird. She took three baths a day, brushed her teeth every time she inhaled deeply, and died a thousand deaths if the lightest activity made her sweat. Now how in the world could you sell her something that would give her yogurt-mouth around a boy?

The biggest danger in building your own wall out in the meadow is that you forget to go back and see what things are like inside the old wall. The Dairy Council forgot that little tidbit the first time around and poured millions of dollars right down the drain.

The second time around they smartened up. They admitted to themselves that milk has a problem within a teenager's wall. So they came up with a setting where the down-side was no longer a problem. Forget being a social drink. Guzzle that milk in private.

Sure, you'll smell bad. But after you brush your teeth and trot out the door, all they'll notice are those glorious breasts and biceps. Now there's a selling point that hits the buyers where they live, inside <u>their</u> wall not yours.

Sometimes you can convert the others and bring them out to the friendly confines of your wall. But don't assume that's automatically the case. As Mohammed is reputed to have said, "If the mountain won't come to Mohammed, Mohammed shall go to the mountain." Never lose sight of reality.

Obviously, it would be nice to pick a winner every time we looked at the Opportunity Model. But as you can see, there are no guarantees. However, we can improve our chances of success by using a number of specific techniques.

I know, I know. I've already said that mindset is more important than techniques. But let me add to that something else. Once you've gotten your mind set in the right direction, specific techniques can be invaluable. After a lifetime of atrophy, explosive thinking needs more than a pep talk. If it's going to blossom, it needs a little specific assistance as well. Just realize something very important; the specific techniques we are about to discover all take place within the context of the Opportunity Model, which is the anchor for our creative efforts.

Moving On

You've had about all the conceptual material you can absorb without hurting yourself. So now it's time to switch gears. The cookbook approach to creativity will begin when you turn the page. So, as they say in Indy ... "Gentlemen, start your engines."

End Note
1. Igor H. Ansoff, "Strategies for Diversification", <u>Harvard Business Review</u>, September-October, 1957, p. 114

7
JUMP STARTING THE BRAIN
(SOME TRIED AND TRUE TECHNIQUES)

This chapter is dedicated to jump-starting the brain. It offers a list of tried and proven techniques and mental gimmicks that can help you become an explosive thinker.[1] After you've tried them on for size we'll move into some newer and more advanced techniques in the next chapters.

Find the #@$#!! Target

I started this book with the fan story for a reason. It's a classic example of problem definition - which is the act of finding the target for all your creativity. Without it, the rest of your creative efforts are wasted. You'll remember that my wife, redefined fan cleaning as soaking, rather than scrubbing. In the process she ran out into the meadow and built a brand new wall of rationality for other people to play in.

It was exactly the same kind of action taken by Einstein, Plato, Newton and the host of luminaries who have molded the development of culture, religion and industry. These re-definitions, these new walls are absolutely crucial to society, because they unleash the functional innovations that move society and individuals ahead by leaps and bounds. When you look at it that way, it does change the apparent importance or your own work, doesn't it? Fan cleaning doesn't look like much until you realize that Susie's creativity freed me up enough to write this book. Without her, I'd probably be scrubbing window screens with a straight pin rather than changing the course of western civilization. And now, you can do the same. All you have to do is digest several steps.

FIRST, discover what the current definition of the problem is. That's often harder than it might seem. After all, I wasn't able to articulate to Susie that I had adopted a scrubbing paradigm as it pertained to ventilation machinery. I just told her I was trying to clean the fan. And no one could tell Newton that they had adopted a theological explanation for physical phenomena; they just prayed fervently every time an apple fell. You need to do a little Content Analysis to discover the current definition.

1. **Look for repeated words or themes.** If folks keep muttering "disaster", "crisis", and "attack", they probably see the situation as a threat, not an opportunity.
2. **Look at the dominant actions.** If they're building forts they're defending against a problem. If they're building tanks, they're getting ready to attack an opportunity.
3. **Look at the tools they've stockpiled.** If you see a lot of shovels, they probably see the situation as a

digging problem. If everyone has their nose stuck to a computer screen, they think it's a numbers problem.

Those are the keys. Susie saw that I had rags, q-tips, bottle brushes, and a toothbrush laid out on the counter when I was fiddling with the fan. That's a pretty obvious give away, regardless of what I say. She also heard me mutter about my finger being too big to **scrub** well, and heard me say "By jiggers, that q-tip **scrubs** like a charm." Once you do a little detective work, the current definition usually pops right out at you. You just have to be patient, and look.

SECOND, remember that the new definition will relate to the current definition in one or more stock ways. It'll be:
- ◆ bigger or smaller,
- ◆ tighter or looser,
- ◆ faster or slower,
- ◆ more abstract or more concrete.

Then you march up and down that stock list of options until something pops. Susie discovered that abstraction was the key. I was scrubbing. But scrubbing is part of a bigger abstraction -cleaning. Aha! At that point she had an anchor and could trot back through the list of stock options again. What are the various ways to clean? She generated a short list of six reasonable ways and soaking happened to be one of them.

THIRD, check your preliminary idea against reality by asking some simple questions.

- "Does soaking, in fact, get rid of dirt?" Susie is a master of the pre-soak cycle on the washing machine.

She knew it would work. So far so good. But another reality check was needed.

- "Is there anything big enough to soak a fan grill?" She was asking herself the Leonardo da Vinci question, "Will existing technology and capabilities allow me to perform this marvelous idea?" That's a key point that sometimes gets lost, much to the chagrin of someone trying to be creative.

- "The bathtub!" thought Susie. "Of course. It'll even hold my husband's bulk. Surely it's big enough for a simple fan grill." That's transference. It is exactly the same logical jump that James Watt made when he borrowed cannon technology to make the first steam boiler.

After that, the whole thing was easy as pie, and since Susie didn't reveal her train of thought until much later I was left in awe at her ability to receive divine revelation. Sometimes redefinition can be as quick and easy as Susie's. Sometimes, however it can be a long and painful process. The impact of an apple didn't really jog Newton into an instantaneous revelation of the entire physical laws of the universe. He actually had to invent his own form of mathematics before he laboriously plodded toward his discoveries. So keep plugging away. Chances are your problem is a little smaller than Newton's.

Reverse Logic

Reverse logic is based on the pompously cynical assumption that everyone else is a fool. If everyone else declares that something is impossible, then the reverse logician is convinced that the thing in question can most certainly be done, and probably quite simply. They think the limits and imperatives that everyone else sees are merely optical illusions. There's a bit of this in every creative, which is what drives them to "boldly go where no man has gone before". If everyone declares that human flight is an impossibility they'll say it's an imperative and invent an airplane out of spite.

Back in 1991 Nickelodeon Studios, a part of Universal Studios in Orlando, was working on a billboard campaign to increase attendance. The prevailing wisdom was that you needed to trigger the "juvenile nag factor" - i.e. - get the kids' attention and get them to nag their parents into coming to the park. But then one creative voice suggested that a "parental revenge factor" might work even better - i.e. - target harried parents instead of kids, and trigger their latent fantasies about wreaking revenge on the cherubs. Suddenly ideas began popping: "Teach your kids some discipline" (with an execution clip from one of its kid shows); "teach your kids some table manners" (with one of its famous green slime shots), "Improve their minds" (with a sloppy scene from its Double Dare show) etc. The general technique here is very straight forward - do the opposite. Just remember that the reverse technique can be applied to any number of entities.

- ◆ **The target market**. Nickelodeon addressed the parents instead of the kids.
- ◆ **The intended outcome**. Punish the kids instead of rewarding them.
- ◆ **The process used**. Go faster instead of slower. Louder, instead of softer. Rev the kids up, instead of keeping them quietly sedated in the back seat.

You'll be surprised at what comes to mind when you change your basic perspective.

Logical Extremes

The logical extremes technique grows out of the concept of reverse logic, and forces us to go beyond the wall. It involves three steps: (1) state a proposition; (2) take it to its logical extreme; then (3) take it to its reverse extreme. An example here might help.

1. **The proposition** - business travelers would rather be at home.
2. **Going toward the logical extreme** - simply involves making a series of statements, each one a little more extreme, as you move from the proposition to, over and beyond the wall of rationality that surrounds it.

Let's take a look at how this might go.

A. Business travelers should only make infrequent day trips so they can spend each night at home (Very tame, still inside the wall).
B. They should never travel more than 20 miles a day on business (Hmmm, you're getting better. Now you're nose to nose with the wall).
C. Business travel should never exceed what you comfortably walk in an hour (Okay, now you're standing atop the wall).
D. Business travel should be unprofitable (Ah, feel the meadow grass, you just stepped over the wall).
E. Business travel should be made unnecessary (Wow. It's kinda fun to play out in the meadow).
F. Business travel should be illegal (Good, the wall is just a dot on the horizon).
G. Business travelers should be shot on sight (I like this. It shows a little emotion as well as creativity).

H. Business travel should be impossible (Bravo. You couldn't find the wall again if you tried).
I. We could crossbreed business people with turtles. That way they could take their homes with them. (I think this puts you in another galaxy. You're not even in the same meadow.)

So where does that get you? Directly, nowhere. But going to the outer limits triggers the germ of an idea that can be tamed and brought back within the wall of rationality for practical use.

When tax breaks on travel and entertainment expense accounts where tightened, the law affected business travel. It made it less profitable. That's pretty close to statement "D" in our series, don't you think?

And what about telemarketing, teleconference calls, computer networks, fax machines, virtual offices, phones and the like. They came about from the absurd notion that business travel could (or should) be unnecessary. Companies are making a mint off that bit of "absurdity". Many of the products, services and ideologies that we take for granted now had their seeds way outside their own contemporary wall of rationality in the beginning.

But those are pretty tame. The real trick is to do something with your weirdest idea, in this case the genetic cross breeding with turtles. Very often your weirdest idea is so weird that it's done nothing but come full circle. Think about Air Force One. What is it? A mobile home. It lets the President be a turtle, doesn't it? In addition, CNN, <u>Time</u> magazine and a host of other organizations have several Winnebago's customized with the comforts of home and office so that field assignments are a bit like taking home with you. Ditto on corporate jets. Some firms even pay the travel expenses for spouses so that the executives never have to leave the soul of hearth and home behind. And several hotel chains, are replacing their rooms with suites in an effort to be more like home than a hotel. In fact, you can even rent a dog for the night at a couple of independents.

3. Going toward the reverse extreme - Next, turn your attention to the logical extreme in the opposite direction. The new proposition would be: business travelers would rather be on the road. The movement to the extreme might include...

   A. take longer, more frequent trips;
   B. make business a constant road trip;
   C. require constant travel from business people
   D. burn all homes;
   E. destroy all offices
   F. shoot anyone found standing still;
   G. eradicate the concept of home or hominess.

Where does that get you? Again, in a direct sense, it gets you nowhere. But when you tame the ideas and haul them back inside the wall, some creative actions occur. Many Fortune 500 firms made home ownership an illusion long ago. They became real estate brokers for their employees, buying from those who'd been transferred out and reselling the properties to those who'd been transferred in. In effect, the employees had only been renting, but they got an equity bonus when they moved. The firms may not have actually destroyed the concept of, or ability to have, a home. BUT, they radically altered the whole concept of home and hominess didn't they?

Inside-Out Thinking

The ideas generated for the Nickelodeon billboards show what can happen when you look at problems from a different perspective. Usually we view buyers from the outside, looking in. Consequently we look for ways that we can invade the buyer and work our magic --- sneak the message in to the kids and get them to nag. But if we crawl inside the car and look around we find that there might be demand factors screaming to get out. Instead of invading their turf, we could orchestrate their escape. Imagine yourself as Mom or Pop on vacation with Jimmy the tormentor, Rachel the whiner, and Freddie, who's better at being grumpy than the 5th dwarf. In all frankness, parents are prone to have less than noble thoughts after a couple of days of this kind of torture. Daydreams of "forgetting" one in a gas station restroom or unmade motel bed flit across the mind. Nobility gives way to survival, and revenge leaves a speculative taste at the back of the tongue. It is nectar. But parents can't act on that and still be a competent, accepting parents. So they'll settle for an acknowledgement of their struggle for civility, a momentary release, a break from the kids. The new billboard supplies it. Gruesome but funny, it gives the release, triggers a humorous threat, a laugh and then a change of plans. The whole role structure and nature of the decision process is changed and the parents become the happy instigators of the visit rather than the grudging targets of childish nags. Besides, a lot of parents growl a preemptive "no" at the first hint of a nag.

Benefit Search

I don't buy a haircut when I go to the barber shop. I buy good looks (or the hope thereof). I'm not interested in the features (47,632 hairs trimmed to the uniform length of

2.17 inches). What I care about is the benefit (a second look from women, acceptance from men).

Once you crawl inside someone's head you need to ask yourself what do they really want. You can do the obvious and ask them directly, with proper credit going to adages about a horse's mouth. And sometimes they'll actually be able to tell you. But many times they won't, because much of the time people simply can't articulate what they really want. So you have to do a little detective work. See what complaints keep surfacing. See what other products they use in conjunction with yours. Those are usually incorporated to supply the benefits your product doesn't. So if Swanson finds out that 80% of its customers add salt to their pot pies, what insightful product modification do you think Swanson should consider? Hmmm? Sometimes creativity is a no-brainer.

Outside-In Thinking

Did you ever notice how clear and obvious a problem is when it's reported by outsiders such as <u>Business Week</u>, <u>The Wall Street Journal</u> or a consultant? Everything boils down to simple black and white.

- ◆ Sears lost massive revenue because it refused to carry national brands.
- ◆ The Edsel bombed because its research was out of date.
- ◆ Corfam failed because DuPont forgot that even imitation leather has to breathe.

If we assume that the manufacturers were not purposely self-destructive, we're left to wonder how the executives missed all these facts that were so obvious to the outsiders. The answer is that outsiders have better vision for the simple reason that they are <u>out</u>side. They don't get caught up in the details. Their thinking isn't clouded by the trauma of impending failure. They don't have to protect their turf. And they don't have to suck up to the boss. They can call a spade a spade, without pretending it looks kinda like a diamond or heart. And they can deal that spade openly for all to see.

Now, you could pay through the nose to bring me in as an outside consultant, and I strongly encourage you to do so. But before you do that, you might want to play outsider yourself. Here's how. Act like a doctor; if it helps, spend $25 to buy a stethoscope and white lab coat (but wear it in private so folks don't think you're weird). Then write the kind of distant and pithy diagnosis a doctor would.

- A doctor doesn't scream, "My God! Mom's turning blue! She can't catch a breath! She's gasping from the agony in her chest! The suffering is unbelievable!"
- Instead, a doctor writes, "56 year old white female, parent to the physician, exhibits classic symptoms of angina, including shallow breathing, chest pains and discoloration."

We hate that uncaring sterility. But ask yourself this. If you were the 56 year old white female in question, which person would you want on the other end of the scalpel? The doctor's emotional distance allows him to make a clear-headed diagnosis. It also puts him in a position to take useful action, because he's not panicked. The same can be true for you, if you can discipline yourself to step outside the situation and take a dispassionate look.

Role-Switch Thinking
Tell you what. Since you're into role playing now, let's keep going. About 90% of the time, creativity involves an

attempt to change the behavior of other people. We're trying to get customers to buy something, pay more or shop on Sundays. We're trying to get employees to work harder, faster or smarter. Or we're trying to get a spouse to take out the garbage or share the covers. So we keep working on something that will move them in the direction we want. But we usually do that by sitting in our own little world trying to impose something on them from arm's length. It's classic "we-them" thinking. What we need to do is crawl over our wall, shimmy through no-man's land, and sneak inside their wall. Then we can turn around and take a look back at our wall. You'd be surprised what it looks like from the other person's perspective. What we call steadfastness may look like obstinacy from their point of view. Our "great deal" might seem like a scam. And our incentive system may look like a cheesy attempt to buy them off. If it helps, go stand outside their office building, home or bedroom. Or dress like them for an hour. You might just be surprised by what you see. Just don't get arrested.

Cocktail Avoidance

My observation is that about 60% of decisions are based on how they'll play at the next cocktail party. We all want to impress people. And none of us wants to be embarrassed. So there's a tendency to base our decisions on what others will think, instead of being based on the facts of the situation. Take a good look at yourself in the mirror. If the cocktail syndrome is getting in the way, stay home once in a while. It'll clear the mind.

Vacuuming

A parachutist on his first jump couldn't get his chute to open. As he plummeted to earth he was passed by a man going the other way. "Do you know anything about parachutes?" he shouted. "Yeh," replied the man going up. "But do you know anything about gas stoves?"

Vacuuming involves sucking information from any source we can find. The problem is we often treat it as a luxury item and stop doing it when we need it most, like when we're plummeting to earth in crisis. More often than not we can unlock the secrets of the universe simply by asking someone. Ask and listen. Be a vacuum, and suck the brains of everyone you meet. People love a good audience, and usually unload their own ideas in response. After all, they're looking for someone who will declare their own scribbles to be refrigerator art. So in addition to making yourself popular, you'll learn something too. All Thomas Edison did was travel to Rensselaer and ask Professor Henry Rowland a few questions. Rowland dumped his guts and Edison walked away with everything he needed to deliver electric current from generator to light bulb. So if you want to be creative, start acting like a vacuum cleaner. Read until your eyes smart. Talk to people. Observe everything around you. And watch TV; if you take an occasional look at something besides prime time fare you may find a gem or two.

Plugging Away

Lest you get the sense that there is a magic button involved in all this, we need to point out that regardless of what gimmicks and crutches you use, your biggest asset is what you sit on. It's the ability to put your fanny in place and focus on the issue at hand, but for how long? Keith Reinhard, Chairman of the DDB Needham advertising agency, started out as a copy writer working on 26 humorous radio ads. When he asked his boss how long he should keep at it, his boss responded, "Until you laugh." That's a very key point.

Take your eye off the clock and keep working until something pops.[2]

Serendipity

Now I'll jump the fence and tell you that creativity can also be instantaneous, via serendipitous revelation; those odd quirks that suddenly hit you in the face. Alexander Graham Bell was having a devil of a time trying to make the telephone work because he couldn't find a mechanism to conduct electricity as desired. Frustration set in, until he noticed his depressed assistant absentmindedly plucking a spring. Bell made a new design built around the vibrating spring, which led directly to "Come here Watson, I need you."[3] And when Percy Spencer, a Raytheon scientist, was tinkering with a radar tube in 1942, he noticed that a chocolate bar in his pocket had melted. Bingo! The microwave oven was born.[4]

Don't get trapped in a maze of self imposed rules and miss the easy insights. That's why it's important to relax. Tense people miss the revelations.

What About Group Techniques?

To this point, we've been treating creativity as though it happens within the confines of your head alone. But most of us work in a group of some kind. So it would be wise to look at several techniques that have worked within an organizational setting.

Brainstorming

Everyone has heard the word "brainstorming". And most people toss it around, even if they've never tried it. But what is it? Well, it's an idea-dump performed by a small working group. The only goal is to generate as many relevant ideas as possible. The only rule is that no criticism is allowed. A specific question is placed before a group, such as "what bothers shoppers most about grocery stores?" and then the floor is thrown open to observations and ideas, each one being recorded, but none being discussed in depth. Ideas start to flow, building on one another and fluctuating between problems and solutions. At the end of an hour, which is about as long as you want to go, the board is filled with ideas. Everything is quick, intense and enthusiastic.

But that's the easy part. The real question is what do you do with that board full of raw thoughts and observations? If you don't make some sense of it, the whole experience is just entertainment - not creativity. So put on your detective hat and look for patterns. And as you do so, be especially mindful of two important ones: **connections** and **surprises**.

- ◆ A good place to start is to highlight the surprises. Did someone mention a problem you'd never heard of? Did someone claim that one of your product's strong points was actually a drawback? Did someone seriously suggest an opportunity or idea that you know is absurd? Or did someone throw up an observation that seemed totally unrelated to the discussion? Circle them all. Any one of them could be the key that unlocks things.

- ◆ Then look for connections between specific problems and specific solutions. Some of these will have to be consciously connected during the original discussion, but others will become apparent as you study the material after everyone else has gone home.

♦ Next, look for the "2-birds with 1 stone" connections. The same problem may be causing more than one symptom. The same solution may solve more than one problem.

♦ Also, look for spillover connections. Solving one problem may actually cause another one, or make an existing problem worse.

♦ Finally, you may want to disassemble the whole thing and separate the thoughts into categories, such as problems and solutions, or strategy and tactics, or personnel and finances, or sex and romance if you're working on the personal level. Then look for connections and surprises within each of the categories. Make sure to note the surprises and connections between categories, because many ideas will fit into more than one category. That alone might tell you something interesting.

Boot Camping

This technique is the mirror image of brainstorming. In fact, it's the ugly half sister. The goal is to lock people in a room and keep working them so hard that exhaustion will finally free the brain. Like brainstorming, the process starts with a specific question. But at that point it parts company. A session can last anywhere from 3 to 16 hours. Quick, enthusiastic intensity is killed at the door.

Ideas are not allowed to be "popped and posted" as in brainstorming. Instead, criticism is demanded, usually microscopically. When a shortcoming is found the group has to find a solution, and the process repeats itself endlessly, because no idea is ever perfect.

The odd thing here is that the original question isn't really important. What you're looking for is the toss-off pearl that will occur in desperation and fatigue, like "I don't know. I can't think anymore. Heck, I can't even sit up straight. Why don't we just call it 'Walkman' and call it a day?" [5]

Floating

Brainstorming is usually fun. Boot camping rarely is. The two approaches also differ in terms of closure. Brainstorming is sometimes seen as too quick, and therefore superficial. Boot camping is usually seen as too slow and painful. Therefore a middle ground, such as "floating", is sometimes used.[6] The goal is to develop general perceptions and ideas rather than specific solutions. So discussion floats along like a raft on a slow river, with a gentle nudge here and there to move it in a useful direction. A typical session is at least 3 hours long, and starts at the most ambiguous and abstract of levels, relying on fatigue to trigger specific ideas as participants look for closure so that they can go home.

- ◆ The process starts with an abstract topic. If you want to replace traditional housing with a cheaper and better alternative, you might start by talking about enclosures in general.

- ◆ Discussion follows this lead, and participants might start talking about caves, bird nests, bear hugs, clam shells, turtle shells and the like.

- As the discussion leader you provide an occasional nudge by asking questions. Maybe you ask them how enclosures for individuals differ from enclosures for groups. Or you ask them to find the one thing that caves, nests and shells have in common.

- After the participants chew on that for a while you ask other questions that increasingly narrow the focus until you zero in on the things that nature could teach architects about enclosures.

By that point, someone floats into the revelation of the self-supporting vaulted ceiling - i.e. - the geodesic dome. So this "flaky" technique (which looks like an embarrassing waste of time to many executives) can generate some very sophisticated and profitable ideas. Not bad, huh?

Attribute Listing

The previous methods can generate tremendous creativity. However, their success depends on the participants' comfort with using them. They're all a little odd, especially floating. And some people feel so foolish using them that they sabotage the process. So, you may want to try something tamer, such as attribute listing. This technique entails intellectually breaking a problem, product or opportunity into its component attributes. Take a hammer for instance. Some of its attributes are:
- used for striking;
- used for pulling;
- manually operated;
- powered by a lever action; and
- has a solid head and a shaft.

The group can participate in listing the attributes, or it can kick into gear after the attributes are listed. The goal is to play around with changing the attributes in various combinations until a good cohesive idea emerges.

You could alter the action from manual lever action to automated torque action, putting the hammer's head on a fly wheel. You could lengthen or shorten the handle to provide varying degrees of torque and controllability. There are any number of options which surface, and they are aided by keeping a checklist of standard options, such as: enlarge, shrink, change shape, alter use, substitute, reverse, combine, multiply, divide, add, eliminate etc.[7] This is nothing more than a step by step guide to idea modification. But it can lead to a very nice array of new ideas, and it's a lot less threatening to executives than the floating technique.

Morphology

This technique is a close cousin to attribute listing, simply incorporating a wider frame of reference. Instead of focusing on a specific product, service or idea, morphology focuses on that item in its broader context. The question might be stated as "How can I steal something without getting caught?" The important components would be:

   (a) What gets stolen (ideas, objects, money, things etc)
   (b) From whom, (a friend, a firm, a supplier, a seller)
   (c) By whom or what (you, another, a machine, nature)
   (d) Methods of evasion (silence, distractions, hiding)

The answers to such questions might lead to a machine that unobtrusively uses the laws of physics to steal TV signals - a tiny satellite dish.[8]

Forced Associations

This technique forces the group to consider a product, service or idea that might arise from the combination of an arbitrary list of things. Combine a gym shoe with the cast you will wear if it doesn't work, and you get "the pump", a popular shoe introduced in 1990. Or combine gym shoes with going barefoot, and you get the Etonic Catalyst, the double soled shoe that lets you pivot on heel or toe, almost like going barefoot. Or combine watching TV with going outside to play, and come up with just about every computer game invented in the past 15 years. Now you tell me ... what would you get if you combined an office desk with what its occupant would rather be doing instead?

Moving On

It's interesting to see the twists of mind that have led to success. It's entertaining to watch the mental gymnastics that some folks go through on their way to glory. And if you're like most readers, your reaction may start with awe then move to, "What's so special about this stuff? I can do that." If you end up at that place, congratulations. That is <u>exactly</u> the point of this book. You <u>can</u> do this stuff. We all have the seed of creativity within us. All we have to do is let it out.

Just don't fall into the trap of discounting a skill because you possess it. Some people actually do that. They say that a certain activity can't really be creativity, because they can do it, and they're not creative. That's a little like Groucho Marx saying he never wanted to join a club that would accept him as a member. Lighten up for goodness sake. If you learn to accept your own gifts, they will grow to the point where you can be proud of them.

Other Techniques

So far, our how-to section reads like "Dr. Anderson's 8 Easy Steps to Wealth and Glory". But wait, as the Ginsu ad says, there's more. We've just scratched the surface. This chapter rolls out the easy stuff. I've saved the tougher techniques for the following chapters. I do that for a reason. It's easy for people to get overwhelmed by creativity, because self-confidence is a central ingredient for it ... and we've been trained in humility, not cockiness.

So one of the goals of this book has been to usher you, step by step, into the mindset of Winston Churchill. At one pre-election cocktail party a matron tried to teach him a little humility by publicly telling him she would be voting for his opponent, Clement Attlee, because he was so humble. Unfazed by the insult, Winnie responded with a smile, "Ah yes madam. And he has so much to be humble about." Churchill was probably the most egotistical man in the 20th century, and with good reason. He was a competent scholar of the classics, a battle tested war veteran, a stone mason, an artist, an historian, an author, a consummate orator, a brilliant politician, and the Prime Minister who literally saved an empire. If there was a problem, he knew down in his gut that he would find the most creative solution available. And he was not bashful about announcing this fact to one and all, which rubbed some people the wrong way. You need a little bit of that kind of chutzpa to be creative. Hopefully your confidence has reached that level by now, because what follows will get a bit more complex.

End Notes

1. *In truth, the various techniques have come from so many sources that it resembles a process of osmosis. However, in an effort to pass appropriate credit to other thinkers, I would note that a number of the ideas are contained in, or suggested by, <u>Source Book for Creative Thinking</u>, ed Sidney J. Parnes and Harold F. Harding (New York: Scribner's 1962) pp. 274-275 and J. Huizinga, <u>Homo Iudens</u>, (Boston: Deacon Press, 1950).*

2. *Interestingly enough, Reinhard's story is related in an advertisement for the <u>Wall Street Journal</u>, in <u>Adweek's Marketing Week</u>, May 29, 1989, pp. 14-15.*

3. <u>People's Chronology</u>, *James Trager, ed., (New York: Holt, Rinehart and Winston, 1979) p. 557*

4. *"A Microwave of the Future, 1964", <u>Wall Street Journal</u>, September, 15, 1989*

5. *Alex F. Osborn, <u>Applied Imagination</u>, 3rd edition, (New York: Scribner's, 1963) pp 286-287*

6. *Floating can be found in <u>Source Book for Creative Thinking</u>, ed Sidney J. Parnes and Harold F. Harding (New York: Scribner's 1962) pp. 274-275. However, they call floating "Synetics".*

7. <u>Source Book for Creative Thinking</u>, *ed Sidney J. Parnes and Harold F. Harding (New York: Scribner's 1962) pp. 240-253*

8. *Edward M. Tauber, "HIT: Heuristic Ideation Technique - A Systematic Procedure for New Product Search" <u>Journal of Marketing</u>, January 1972, pp. 58-70*

8
NIGHT VISION
(LEARNING TO SEE IN THE DARK)

The previous chapter involved a push-button approach to creativity, based on concrete actions. The techniques all centered around quick and simple things we can <u>do</u> to change our mental perspective and open a few windows on new ideas. They're wonderful techniques, and they work well no matter how many times they've been done before.

But just about every organization has at least one person who's already been exposed to them. So if you want a competitive edge mentally, you need to push beyond the usual techniques. In addition, the world is a complex place that changes daily. As a result, things can get pretty foggy on the other side of the wall. So what you <u>do</u> and what you <u>think</u> has to be based on your ability to <u>see</u>.

In short, Chapter 6 taught you how to think; this chapter will teach you how to see. It's about developing creative vision; and to do that, we have to move from the concrete world into the subjective. That can be a frightening step if you've spent your whole adulthood dealing with the concrete world of numbers, facts and data. So let's start by getting rid of the fear.

When I was in graduate school, the faculty wanted students to do the most complex linear programs, factor analyses, and other mathematical functions by hand. Officially, this was so we'd understand what went on inside computers, instead of seeing them as a magic black box. Unofficially, we suspected it tied in with the $10 million grant proposal the school had recently submitted for state of the art computing facilities. It seemed they were making sure students expressed a high need for the machines when polled by the donor board. Personally, it almost destroyed several people, because the teachers made the natural complexity so much worse. Just before they launched into their incomprehensible spiels on numerology, each professor would announce,

"This material is actually very easy.
I'm almost embarrassed to put you all through it."

They were using denial as an attempt to eliminate fear. Predictably, the opposite occurred. Those of us without tape on the bridge of our glasses were not only left in the dust, but we were also made to feel that comprehension was beyond us forever, since we were so stupid. After all, this stuff was supposed to be easy.

I promised myself then and there I'd never do that to anyone else (except maybe a computer professor now and then). You can't eliminate fear by denying the existence of its cause. The only way to eliminate fear is to acknowledge the difficulty of the task, and help people master it. So let me make an announcement up front --- you might find the material in this chapter very difficult. If so, that's because the material is difficult. So don't get worried about your abilities. Just relax, it'll come. And I'm going to be right here, giving you a hand.

The Abstract Vault

Charles Revson, the father of Revlon Cosmetics, once said, "In the factory we mix chemicals; but in the store we sell hope."[1] That quote may raise your feminist hackles a bit, but realize that Revson performed an abstract vault of marvelous dimensions. He elevated his vision enough to find out what was really going on in the minds and lives of his customers. A woman isn't buying pastel red # 632-PV1993. She's buying beauty, popularity, acceptance, professionalism, romance or any of the other fantasies that make it worth getting out of bed in the morning. Once you understand that, you have a chance of succeeding; a chance of generating new ideas that might capture her imagination, loyalty and money.

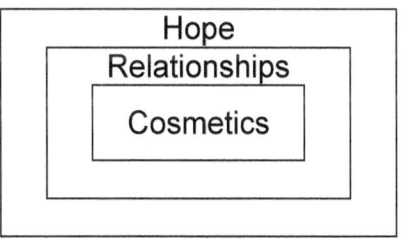

Most of us stand so close to our respective tree that we never get to see the entire forest. Revson ascended to a vantage point where he could see not only the tree of his brand of makeup, but also the forest itself - the history of human relations.

First, Revson uncovered the importance of the future. Women base their decisions, not on the present, but on what could, might or should happen tomorrow. As the Apostle

Paul indicated, hope is the belief in something that has not yet occurred. Consequently the notion of ongoing beauty therapies, ongoing benefits and future payoffs became a marketing mainstay.

Second, Revson realized that hope extends far beyond physical appearance. It also addresses acceptance, romance, success, tranquility and the other issues that inhabit and fuel basic human nature.

After that, marketing cosmetics was a fairly easy task. You didn't just focus on the woman's looks. You focused on the <u>impact</u> of her looks: on self image, getting the guy, the job, the accolades of the crowd and the respect of her friends.

And lest I be accused of sexism, let me hasten to add that the same approach works on men. I don't go to Home Depot to buy hardware. I go to buy competence. They have those guys in orange aprons who will give me expert advice on how to do every job around the house, and keep me from looking like a schlemiel in front of my wife and kids. They do that because they understand something that's very important; a man doesn't really buy a 1/4 inch, cross loop carbide tip drill bit, model number 25icl-cb-db1993. He buys hassle free holes.

Okay. So how, exactly do you do the abstract vault? Start by imagining your product, issue or problem as resting inside the smallest of a nested set of boxes. Then ask yourself, "What's the next biggest box?" You do that by asking: "Why is this an issue?" or "What is the person trying to do?" or "What causes thus and such to occur?" Keep going until you find the "big box" - the one that explains the bulk of behavior and possibilities relative to your problem. Notice - you keep vaulting over the wall of each box, and each vault makes the issue one step more abstract. Hence the name - Abstract Vault.

Allegorical Thinking

Allegorical thinking is the search for metaphor: i.e. "driving a car is like ...." This technique is one of the ways in which creative people can rise from the specific to the abstract level. Fishing is a popular allegory for marketing itself, and has given rise to a number of concepts, like: luring the customer into a store, trolling for prospects, bait and switch, and the like. Allegories help us see things at the abstract level, thereby freeing our minds to roam.

Some of the most successful people on the after-dinner speaker's circuit have traditionally been football coaches. They have great celebrity stories to tell and wallow in name dropping. But the real reason for their success is that the vast majority of males in the audience buy the allegory that "life is a lot like football". There is a lot of truth to that cliché, but the allegory approach isn't confined to boyhood sports. It also works in the gentler realms as well.

> Courtship is a lot like a staged musical, complete with: romantic backdrops, choreography, song and dance, telling entrance and exit lines, and good rhythm.

> Cabinet making is a lot like making bread. No two projects ever come out exactly the same. Working the wood by hand and kneading dough both have the sensation of molding a living object. And both have a distinctive aroma that bespeaks home and hearth.

So where does all this allegory get you? It triggers creativity. Once a stumbling adolescent grasps the courtship allegory he turns into a dangerous Lothario. He develops good lines. He knows the power of mood music and lighting. And he knows how to script the entire evening, right down to who sits where when the big move occurs. And when the baker grasps the woodworking allegory, he becomes the premier wedding caterer, master of the seven-tier cantilevered wedding cake.

Try it yourself. Say, "My job (task, product etc) is a lot like ... " and see where it leads. If your answer is the old tried and true, "a pain in the ass" then go with the obvious. Think like a proctologist and see what happens.

Historical Allegory

Historical allegory is a subset of the previous technique, but separate enough to warrant a word. Back in 1974 a major fast food chain was experiencing terrible problems with its franchise owners running around like loose cannons. They introduced unauthorized menu items, dealt with unauthorized suppliers, ran unauthorized promotions, refused to comply with corporate directives and constantly attacked the home office for more autonomy. A deluge of major lawsuits cascaded through the courts and the home office was in disarray. The problem was made worse by the fact that the rebellion was being led by the earliest franchisees, who'd also become near and dear friends of the chain's founder. The founder, though not dead, was in his dotage and upper management, therefore, felt paralyzed. They tried conferences, pep talks, harping, visiting consultants, incentive systems, the works. Nothing helped.

That's where I came in. I was the most junior member of my consulting firm and had been booted out of the conference room because my boss was negotiating our fee. I was cooling my heels in the hall when the Operations VP stopped for a chat and unburdened himself about his travails.

As his tale of woe unfolded, I thought of Winston Churchill during World War II. He had sent British troops to their sure death in the lost cause of defending Greece from the Nazis because, as he said, you must support and/or punish your dearest friends above all others or your credibility evaporates. What an odd allegory I discovered. Fast food is like Greece (not grease, you heretics).

Steeled by Churchill's example, the vice president arbitrarily canceled the first three franchises when they came up for renewal two months later. Shock waves exploded throughout the system as franchisees realized that not even the founder's bosom buddies were immune from million-dollar discipline. The lawsuits were withdrawn, obedience became the norm, and the franchisees went even further. They suggested, supported and financed a complete renovation of every store, in spite of the fact that they didn't own the land or buildings themselves. It's a nice example of the combination of creativity and raw power in business. It's also a great illustration of how I can be exploited. That was probably the best single piece of consulting work I ever did, and I didn't get a dime for it. But I did get one heck of an example, didn't I?

Mind Mapping

Mind mapping is actually a synthesis of the other methods: redefining situations, reversing logic, moving to the abstract level, and crawling toward solutions via inside-out and logical extremes.[2] By way of example, put yourself in Cover Girl's shoes. What can you say about eye shadow, mascara and liner that hasn't already been said? What could you tap into that would provide you with a competitive edge in the mind of the consumer? That's a toughie. But let's use mind mapping and see where it takes us.

An overview - A mind map is the tangible representation of stream-of-consciousness thinking, which constantly branches, rejoins and branches once again. It gets very complex, but it starts from a very simple point - a proposition.

Let's take a scrap of paper we found behind a copywriter's wastebasket. It has a phrase that apparently got rejected as an advertising tag line, but it makes a decent initial proposition.

> *The Lady has eyes.*

As you stare at that phrase, realize two things. First, you don't have enough room to work. In fact, it is best to start your mind map in the middle of an immense chalk board so that your ideas don't prematurely cease upon reaching the edge of the board. Our space limitations in a book format really don't do it justice. Consequently, we'll have to do this in stages, and be very selective, showing only bits and pieces of the whole thing. Second, mind mapping is reminiscent of diagramming a sentence. Junior high <u>did</u> prepare you for this aspect of creativity, so send your old teacher a thank you note. The procedural steps in mind mapping are like a very structured brainstorming session:

1. Write down a proposition.
2. Record the initial impressions as they come to mind and attach them to the proposition, or each other.
3. Go back to each impression and write in the specific thoughts, questions and observations it triggers.
4. Repeat at a deeper level
5. Keep repeating until fatigue shuts down your brain, or some brave soul cries "enough".
6. Then go back and study the map. Look for:
    a. Patterns ---- Oddities
    b. Interesting insights - the grand "aha"

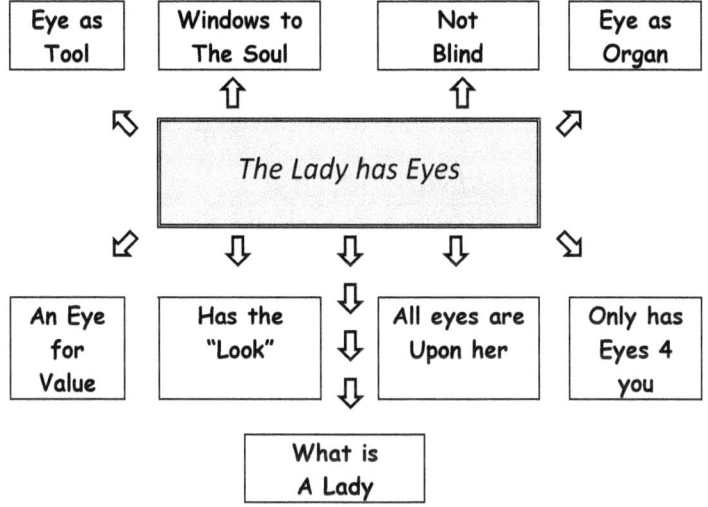

Generating initial impressions - Take a look at the initial impressions that can arise from the proposition. Notice that these impressions can range all over the conceptual map. Some are purely functional (eye as an organ, an eye for value), some are cultural (what is a lady), some are relational (only has eyes for you, all eyes are upon her) and some relate to issues of status and control (**the** lady, power, eye as tool).

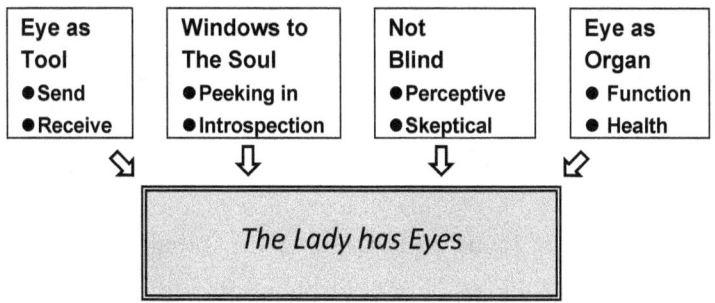

Going for depth - The next step involves generating questions, thoughts and observations relative to each of the original impressions. An explosion of issues usually occurs in this step. I've truncated the following graphics just to save space, but I think you get the idea.

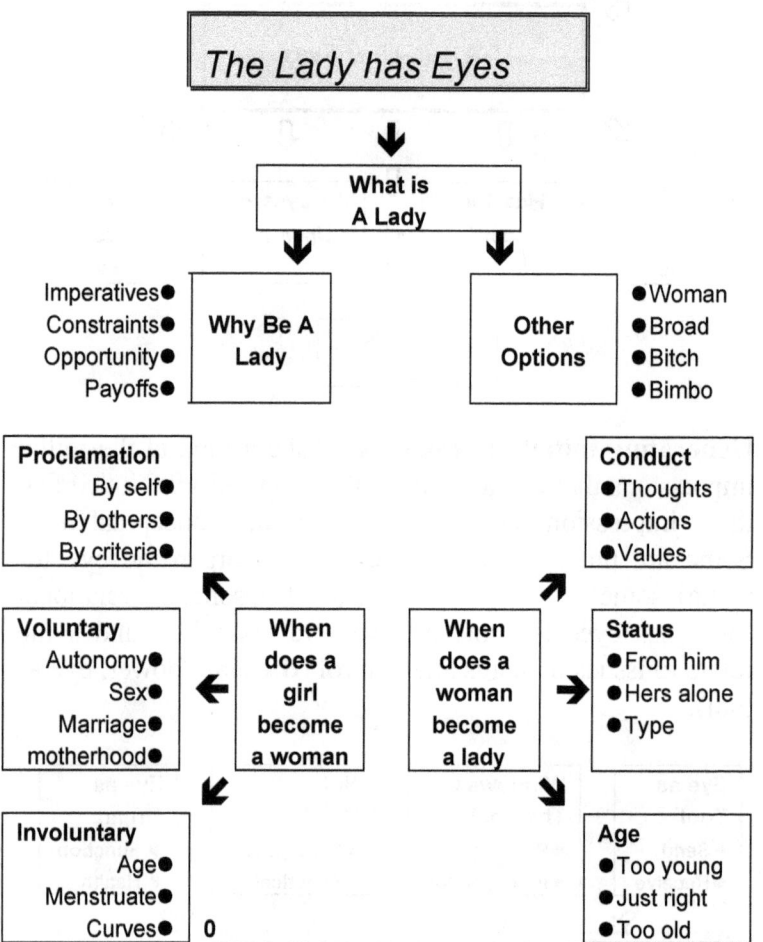

Finally, you can focus on just one of the initial impressions (What is a lady) and expand on it. Notice that as soon as you focus on one avenue, thoughts come in a flood. Study the figure for a moment and you'll probably be able to add still more. As you do, realize that each and every one of the initial impressions gives rise to a diagram at least as extensive as the one shown. In fact, the "all eyes are upon her" impression is a veritable gold mine of "who, what, when and why" issues.

Some observations on mind mapping - There is no "right" way to do mind mapping. Some people prefer to do it in the fashion we've described. Others like to generate one initial impression, follow it through to exhaustion, then repeat the cycle by generating another initial impression. You could also start with the final snippets of thoughts and observations, then work backwards, force fitting them into impressions and propositions. It doesn't much matter. You use the tool. Don't let it use you. But what does all this work get you?

Ideas. They're sitting right in front of you. Just look at what we generated for Cover Girl - and that was just from one little corner of the Mind Map. It's obvious that Cover Girl's past success has come from making teenage girls feel like grownup women; and subsequently like ladies. Cosmetics are a way to buy apparent maturity and status. But look at something else. Chances are that Cover Girl could also have an impact on adult women as they decide what they want to be (person, woman, lady, broad, bitch, bimbo etc). Sure it's a political powder keg. All the more reason to charge into the fray. Everyone else will be ducking for cover and leaving the battlefield vacant. But as you charge, you better have a good road map of the mine-fields. This technique can give you that map.

Imaging

Gillette has been very successful making razors. So much so, that if America has a "cutting expert" it's them. Then tell me, why they don't also sell scissors, cutlery, surgical equipment, lawnmowers, carpentry saws and harvesting machines?. I'll tell you why. Because they're peeking in your bathroom window, that's why. They're peeping toms, good old fashion voyeurs. They've made a fortune hanging around outside bathroom windows. And you can do the same.

The Imaging Model

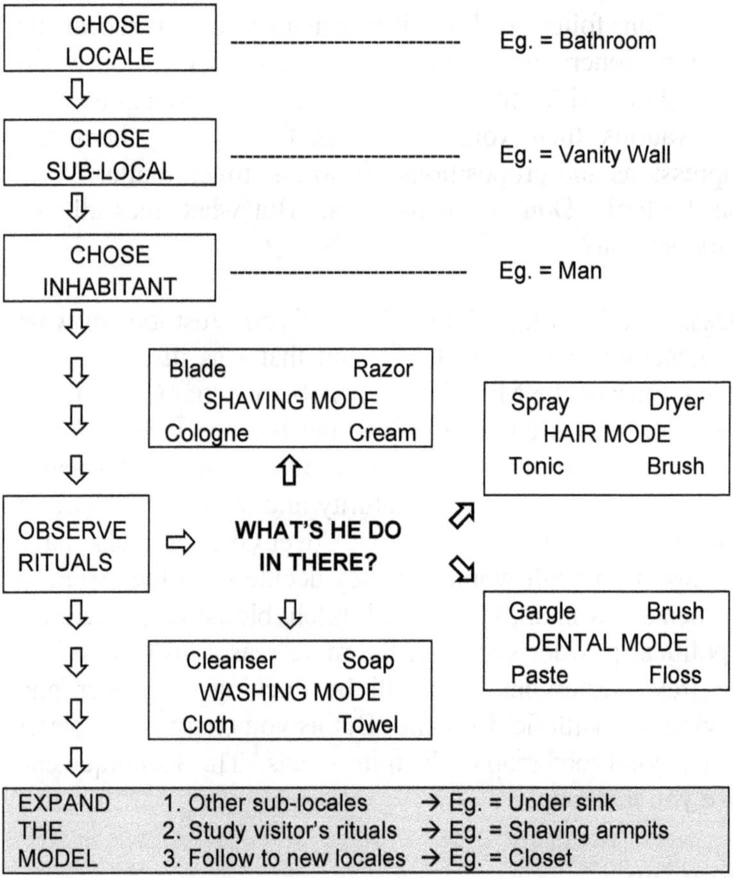

```
┌──────────────┐
│   CHOSE      │  ----------------   Eg. = Bathroom
│   LOCALE     │
└──────┬───────┘
       ⇩
┌──────────────┐
│   CHOSE      │  ----------------   Eg. = Vanity Wall
│   SUB-LOCAL  │
└──────┬───────┘
       ⇩
┌──────────────┐
│   CHOSE      │  ----------------   Eg. = Man
│   INHABITANT │
└──────┬───────┘
       ⇩
```

	Blade Razor	
	SHAVING MODE	
	Cologne Cream	

		Spray Dryer
OBSERVE RITUALS ⇒	**WHAT'S HE DO IN THERE?**	HAIR MODE
		Tonic Brush

		Gargle Brush
	Cleanser Soap	DENTAL MODE
	WASHING MODE	Paste Floss
	Cloth Towel	

EXPAND THE MODEL	1. Other sub-locales → Eg. = Under sink
	2. Study visitor's rituals → Eg. = Shaving armpits
	3. Follow to new locales → Eg. = Closet

1. **Pick a specific physical location in the other person's life.** Just about any place will do, but the best choice is usually the location where you've already got one or two products. For Gillette that was the bathroom, because that's where most razors are kept. In fact, the location was even more specific than that, focusing on the counter and vanity wall of the bathroom. Gillette ignored the toilet and shower. They also ignored anything that went on under the sink.

2. **Keep a close eye on that location, and its major inhabitant.** You'll get immersed in the behavioral rituals, habits and needs of that person, which will reveal a logical progression of new product/service opportunities. By focusing on a man's vanity wall, Gillette had thrown itself into the most active location in a man's life. The kitchen sink is the only place that receives more time and attention in the American home. But most of that time and attention still comes from women. So, if men are the target market, Gillette clearly had the best location.

3. **Watch the behavior with a microscope.** Gillette's location put it in the midst of numerous overlapping behavioral clusters, all occurring at or near the bathroom sink and vanity wall. Just take a look. There are at least 5 different behavioral clusters - with almost 20 different product needs - and it all takes place within a location that is about 3 feet wide. Pretty amazing. Consequently, Gillette has successfully come out with deodorant, hair spray, after shave lotion and cologne, hair dryers and a host of related products. But notice something interesting. They're not related by technological similarity; there's a world of difference between making a razor blade and hairspray. Instead, the products are related by usage patterns, ie, by bathroom rituals.

4. **Look around.** Now that you've gotten the hang of imaging, you're ready to get really creative, because opportunities are passing before your eyes all the time. All you've got to do is look. There are three ways to do this.

A. **Get a little wide eyed**. Wait! What just flashed across the mirror? It was a towel. That doesn't live on the vanity wall. But the guy used it while facing the wall. So it's part of the existing rituals, and therefore fair game. Once you peek at where he hangs it, you'll also see that there's a whole lot more to a bathroom than the vanity wall. Opportunities suddenly appear everywhere you look: the toilet (toilet paper, deodorizers); the shower (soaps, shampoos, shower massagers, shower curtains, wash clothes, towels); under the sink (shoe polish, cleanser); or the general room decor (curtains, rugs, light fixtures, vanities, wall hangings).

B. **Watch for visitors**. This may be a guy's bathroom, but I know I saw a girl in there. Would you look at that? She's using his razor. Oh geez. She's using it in the most interesting places. Come here and take a look. Ohmygod. Don't. She's bleeding like a stuck pig.

Hey. I bet we could make a bundle by coming out with a rounded edge razor that wouldn't catch on all those tendons. Women would love it. We could call it "Lady Gillette". Whadyathink? When newcomers enter the location, keep an eye on them. They have their own rituals and needs, and they may even be more profitable than your original inhabitant. A woman shaves twice as much acreage as a man. She also has about 10 rituals at the vanity wall to the man's measly 5, and each of her rituals involves twice as many products. That little visitor should be promoted to the role of inhabitant and watched like a hawk.

C. **Tag along.** Where's the next place they go? It might just be to the closet. Hey, how about Gillette bathrobes and slippers or a line of dress shirts? Or maybe the next place she stops is her lingerie drawer (Gillette panties?) or her makeup vanity (Gillette cosmetics, now there's a gold mine).

I personally like the imaging technique, for several reasons.

First, it captures my attention with strong visual images. And since attention is an important part of creative thinking, that's very useful.

Second, those visual images let me "see" ideas, in living color, in 3 dimensions and in graphic detail. The situation and my ideas about it aren't just stagnant two-dimensional thoughts.

Third, it focuses my attention on the other person rather than on my own manufacturing technology, and that's always useful.

Finally, it's an easy way to comprehend a very complex situation. Imaging helps me discover the underlying patterns of life. And once I have a handle on those, my creative juices come in a flood. In fact, uncovering the patterns in life is so important that the effort deserves a chapter all its own.

Vision

You started this chapter with an abstract vault. Then you did a little allegorical thinking and mind mapping. And to round out the experience, you learned the joys of voyeurism. I bet your brain is tired right now. You know why? Because it's just been stretched. That's what developing vision is all about. You don't snap your fingers and suddenly have it. You work like a dog to develop it.

I told you this might be a hard chapter. I also told you that's ok. Some things in life are hard. There's also one other thing I didn't tell you. It's ok to re-read a chapter. There's a lot of material in this one, and you can miss a lot of meat the first time through. But why do it?

Ask the first George Bush. He lost an election to Bill Clinton, in part, because he was publicly bewildered by "this vision thing". Lots of executives lose their jobs for the same reason. Wouldn't it be nice if you weren't among them?

Ask your common sense, too. If you're going to vault a wall into the unknown, don't you think a well developed talent for night vision would be helpful?

Wall vaulting is not a simple act of self entertainment. It's a serious business, and creative people do it for a very good reason. They do it because they see something out there in the meadow. Now that you've got the tools, you can come take a look.

End Notes
1. *Revson's quote is cited in, among numerous other places, Positioning: The Battle For Your Mind, by Al Ries and Jack Trout, (New York: McGraw-Hill, 1981)*

2. *Mind mapping has many fathers, however, Mr. Tony Buzan asserts a strong legal claim to the model and it serves as a mainstay of the consulting and educational efforts of his Buzan Centers. For more information you may wish to contact: The Buzan Center, 415 Federal Highway, Lake Park, Florida, 33403; (407) 881-0188, or read Tony Buzan's, Use Both Sides of Your Brain, Dutton Publishing Company, 1974. The model has also been popularized by The Center for Creative Leadership in Greensboro, N.C.*

9
DICK TRACY, WHERE ARE YOU?
(FINDING PATTERNS IN THE TRENCHES)

I had two grandmothers. Essentially, they were identical. Both had two eyes, two ears, two legs, etc. But one got hardening of the arteries and became goofy at age 70. The other stayed crystal clear until she died at 84. After a comparison of diet, medical history and organic problems, I found the cause. Word puzzles. The clear-headed one did a dozen a day. The one who visited her neighbors in the buff did nary a one.

My scientific conclusion: the intellectual work involved in such puzzles exercises the brain and keeps it well practiced in the problem solving skills we need in daily life, whether that's inside the wall, outside the wall or pretending we're one of the bricks. That's what you call two-fisted empirical research.

So let's take a look at how we handle puzzles and see if that knowledge can help us be more creative. The message below is in code. Each letter is a substitute for the real letter, and the substitutions are consistent. In other words, if K represents "w" in one word, it will also represent a "w" every other time it appears.

So, get to work, crack the code, and discover the magic message that will change your life. Go on. Get a pencil. And play fair. Don't read any further until you solve it.

TEBK XII FP PXFA XKA ALKB, MOLDOBPP

____ ___ __ ____ ___ ____, _____

ABMBKAP LK QEB   RKOBXPLKXYIB   JXK.

_____ __ ___ _____ ___.

Statistics tell me that 59.2% of readers always skip ahead to find the answer before they've worked the problem. I'd be upset, except that I sit firmly in that majority myself. So this is your chance to show more moral fiber than the author. Go on, give it a try. The following discussion will make more sense if you do.

* * * * * * *

Okay. Did you solve it? Then let's move on. Although the solution itself imparts a fair bit of wisdom, the real issue for us is <u>how</u> you obtained the solution.

This little puzzle is a lot like life. It's complex; containing 55 separate clues (code letters) and each of them could be any one of the 26 letters in the alphabet. That means you've got 1,430 (55 x 26) possibilities to sift through. And that's just for a simple little two line word problem. Imagine the complexity of raising a child, designing the space shuttle or increasing market share by 9%. Those lead to millions of possibilities. That's a heck of a lot of work.

No wonder 63% of people try to short circuit the search by letting someone else (preachers, politicians, salesmen or authors) tell then the answers. The only problem is, when you punt like that, you put yourself under someone else's thumb. If you let them tell you what life means, you automatically let them tell you what to do about it. So here's a little tidbit for you:

The first step in ceasing to be one of the sheep is to figure out the meaning of life for yourself.

But how do you do that without letting the complexity drive you nuts? You steal a page from Dick Tracy's handy detective manual and realize that you don't have to do all 1,430 (or 6 million) steps. Once you get a system, you can cruise through complexity and zero in on the meaning of life, and the underlying cause of the problems you need to solve. And you can do it in about 10 steps, rather than 1,430. The secret lies in two fairly obvious rules:

> **SIMPLIFY, SIMPLIFY, SIMPLIFY.** Don't stick the whole steak in your mouth at one time. Cut it into little pieces and chew each piece to death.
>
> **LOOK FOR THE PATTERNS.** Life is not random. <u>Every</u>thing has a pattern, whether it's the M.O. of a crook or the developmental pattern of HIV.

Once you figure out the overall pattern, you can work backwards and fill in the details.

Think about this for a minute. I'm suggesting that you work at the extremes: jumping back and forth between the smallest unit of analysis and the biggest - between a single bite of steak and the entire pattern of a cow's existence in the universe. I do that because the vast middle ground of medium sized issues and facts is the trap that forces you to do all 1,430 steps. Let's take a look at how this works on our little word problem, then see if that can teach us anything about dealing with life in general.

1. **Do a vowel search**. In English, every word must have at least one vowel. And there are only 5 vowels (A,E,I,O and U). So starting with a vowel search limits a lot of complexity. You're only looking for 5 letters, not all 26. And when we look at the puzzle, we see that every word contains either an X, B, F, or L. So they probably stand for the four most common vowels (a,e,i, and o). So now we're only worrying about 4 pieces rather than all 55.

2. **Look for one-letter words**. In English, one-letter words <u>are</u> vowels, with the most common ones being A or I. However, a nasty puzzle maker (such as myself) won't give you any one-letter words, because that makes things too easy. So you move up a notch.

3. **Focus on two-letter words.** The most common ones are AT, AN, BE, IS, IT, OF, OR, OK, ON, TO, UP, BY. Now you've got a little context to wrap around those probable vowels. But that may not do a thing for you, so you move up a notch.

4. **Focus on 3-letter words**. Ah ... we finally get a break. The key is the coded word XII. We know that's a vowel

followed by a double consonant. You could run a complete set (abb, acc, add... ebb, ecc, edd ... ibb, icc, idd ... obb, occ, odd ... etc), and you'd come up with some ideas (like add, ebb, and odd). But let's get simple and straight forward. The most common three letter word with a vowel and a double consonant is ... ALL. And since I'm lazy, I figure the puzzle maker is too, so I'll just arbitrarily choose the obvious answer and see where it leads. I assume X=A and I=L and plug those in wherever they appear.

5. **Look for the words nearest completion.** Once you get a letter or two, the puzzle starts to solve itself.

6. **Make controlled guesses**. XKA (a--) looks like a connecting word to me. It's in the midst of a phrase set off by a comma. So what the heck "and" is an obvious choice. And that lets me make K=N and A=D in every word that holds them. Again, the puzzle solves itself.

7. **Look for the new words that just approached completion.** Every letter you solve opens up new words for possible solution, or partial solution. And again, make some educated guesses. If you see "-ion", 9 times out of 10 the "-" will be a "T" or an "S". So go with the obvious and see where it leads you.

8. **Use the process of elimination.** If you've already solved for three of the vowels (B=E, X=A, F=I), what do you think the L stands for? Hmmm? Could it be "O"? Plug it in and see if it works.

9. **Look for a nearly completed phrase.** Commas are your friends. They set apart phrases. And thankfully, a lot of phrases in English are used so often that they have become recognizable clichés --- such as: "when all is

said and done", "when the dust settles", "over the dam", "over the river", "under the bridge", and "under the sun". It just so happens that we've got one of those very clichés in our puzzle, "**--en** all is said and done". And once you solve the phrase you can go back down to individual words and solve for some more missing letters.

10. **Look at the whole message.** I got it! "When all is said and done, --o--ess de-ends on the un-easonable -an". Now think. Oh Yeh! I got it again. "When all is said and done, --o--ess depends on the unreasonable man". Now ... *what* depends on the unreasonable man? Think man. Think. I got it! It's "progress". Congratulations. You just solved the puzzle.

"WHEN ALL IS SAID AND DONE, PROGRESS DEPENDS ON THE UNREASONABLE MAN."

Now notice something very interesting. You were so brilliant that you found the solution without actually solving for every single code letter first. Obviously something very interesting is going on here and it's worth a good look. It's actually the subconscious process that runs at light speed behind the phenomena that Malcolm Gladwell called snap judgments in his popular book, Blink.

The Rules for Pattern Searches

Unless you completely short-circuited, you followed a scenario similar to the one I've mapped out here. It involves a fairly standard set of decision rules that are so much a part of you that you don't really use them consciously.

Rule 1 - Intuition is as important as fact. It may even be more important. If you go back through our 10 steps you'll see that logic was augmented by controlled guessing. In fact, without intuition (that's what controlled guessing is) it would be impossible to solve the puzzle. Every creative problem solver, from Einstein to Martin Luther, has relied heavily on the assumptions and controlled guessing that make up intuition. We just call them hypotheses to impress the boss.

Rule 2 - Check and double check. Guessing by itself is not enough. You always have to double check your assumptions and guesses by looking at the facts. Do things work out? If the message had come out like the one that follows, you'd know something was wrong.

TEBK XII FP PXFA XKA ALKB, MOLDOBPP
When all us saps add time,   trespass

ABMBKAP LK QEB RKOBXPLKXYIB JXK.
tenants   on the   unreasonable   tan.

But what, specifically is wrong?
Facts must be checked at two levels.

◆ The first is **cumulative fact** - i.e. meaning - which is the most important concern. When you put all the little facts together, does the result make sense? This translation fails that test. It makes no sense whatsoever. So we want to find out why.

◆ To do that we need to move down a level and check out **specific facts**. Are all code letters translated with **consistency**? If you take the time, you'll find they are not. Sometimes P=S, and sometimes A=S. And there are several other duplications as well. In addition, even if the translation is consistent, there is the issue of **accuracy**. After all, the guess that J=T is just flat inaccurate, no matter how consistent it may or may not be.

So, to severely paraphrase the Apostle Paul, "These three things abideth for the creative: accuracy, consistency and meaning. But the greatest of these is meaning." Obviously, dealing with facts is more complex than stump politicians would have us believe. This little parlor game is actually the thing that keeps us from committing insane acts based on some nimrod's interpretation of scriptures, constitutions or treaties "commanding" us to wipe out anyone with an unreasonable tan. Think about that for a second, would ya?

AIN'T SCIENCE GRAND? The process of guessing and then checking the facts is nothing more than the process of hypothesis generation and testing. And that folks is the scientific method in a nutshell. So congratulations. You're just as good as all those PhD's locked away in their laboratories.

A Model for Pattern Searches
Now that we've run through an example and established two general rules, let's get a picture and a few step by step instructions.

Step 1 - Start with the smallest unit of analysis, then expand. In our example, you moved from letters to words to phrases to the entire message. Don't be afraid to start small. Victory often lies in the details.

Step 2 - Go with the obvious. The first thing that comes to mind is usually correct. A two-letter word ending in "s" is going to be "is" 99% of the time. So go with it.

Step 3 - Use what you learned in one place to solve a problem in a new place. If X=A in one word, try the same solution everywhere it occurs.

Step 4 - Always check the context and clues you've already created. Every step you take sets the stage for the next step. So don't ignore the work you've already done, even if it seems to lead nowhere at the time. In short, if you're not going to do step 4, don't waste time doing step 3.

Step 5 - Look for patterns. The whole solution rests on your ability to see patterns and meaning. How do letters relate to one another? How do words relate to one another? And ultimately, how do phrases relate to one another?

Without your ability to see patterns, this little problem that entertains 84 year old grandmothers is impossible to solve.

You will also note that this search for relationships is the same thing I counseled when we were analyzing brainstorming data. It all fits together. That's it. The model is nothing more than a guide for jumping back and forth between guessing and proving. There are lots of false starts and mistakes along the way; a lot of grunt work; and a lot of little leaps and revelations as well.

Finally, note that the size of the intuitive leaps gets bigger the closer you get to the final solution. At first you can guess a letter here and there. As you work, you can fill in an entire word at a jump. After more work, an entire phrase suddenly becomes evident. Then at the end, a curtain seems to rise and the entire meaning of the puzzle suddenly becomes crystal clear. That's because <u>you</u> created all the clues.

The Pattern Model

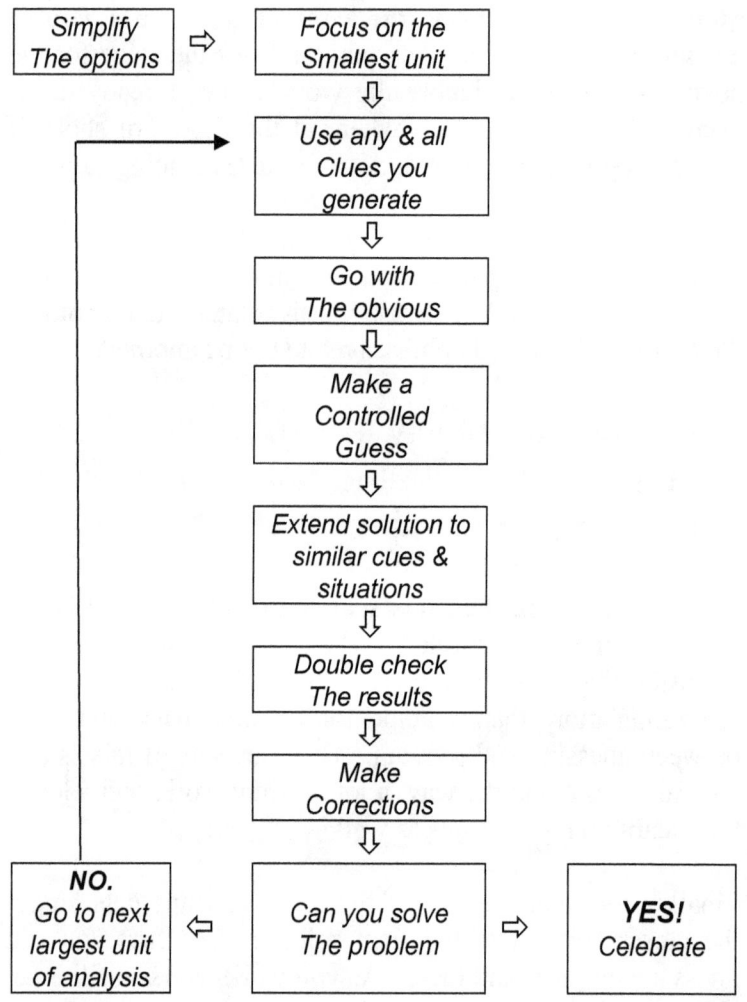

Is All This Really Necessary?

Susie doesn't like this chapter. She says it's unnecessary. That might be true, but I suspect that her reaction grows out of the fact that she was able to solve the entire puzzle in 1 minute and 46 seconds. You see, she works on a Dell word puzzle book in bed every night, so this kind of thing is second nature to her. The rest of us, however, probably don't have that kind of training. So a step by step guide might be useful.

Susie's other criticism of the chapter is that it doesn't reflect the way she solves puzzles. She does, in fact, search for vowels first; but her next step is an uncanny ability to find letter combinations, like "th", "ph" and "qu". After that she just stares at the letters until the words come to her via revelation. My response is, "Bravo".

- ◆ There isn't just one way to solve a puzzle.
- ◆ There isn't just one way to solve a problem.
- ◆ There isn't just one way to be creative.

I've said it once, and I'll say it again. **This book is supposed to stimulate you, not control you**, or force you into someone else's 6 easy steps to success. You hold the key to your own creativity, not me. You also have the ability to come up with techniques that will work better for you than mine will. So the elaborate steps in this chapter simply serve to show you one way to discover patterns. If your way is different, that's terrific. Just do yourself a favor and write down the steps you do use. Then you've got a tried and proven method that you can use to find useful patterns when you're dealing with the very real problems you experience in life.

What About Real Life Problems?

I know. You wonder if there's any practical use for this pattern searching approach. Let me tell you a little story and see what you think. Back in the mid 1970's the baking soda folks at Arm & Hammer noticed that their sales where, how do we say this, a disappointment. Extra advertising didn't do a thing to improve the situation. A steady stream of industry analyses, market research, and competitive assessments gave them a healthy dose of information overload, but little else.

> *<u>DATA</u> – <u>DATA</u> –<u>DATA</u> --- <u>DATA</u> – <u>DATA</u>*
> *More women were working. There were fewer kids under 12, so fewer cookies eaten. Working parents don't have time to really clean house. Grandma was stuffed in an old folks home, but her advice was still available. Each kid eats 17 cookies per week. Mothers weren't home to bake those after-school cookies. All they wanted was something quick & easy to mask the problems and clean up the obvious messes. She used to have loads of old wives' remedies, like removing tea stains with baking soda. Nobody was watching the kids. In fact, they weren't home to do a lot of things. But cookies only use 1 lousy teaspoon of baking soda per batch anyway – so who cares? My mom wore tennis shoes. Mom needed Grandma's help. Imagine the smell in their refrigerator, laundry hamper, rugs, etc. Is there any function that uses more than 1 teaspoonful of soda at a time??? They had lots of money to spend but no time.*

So they went back to the drawing boards in a process very similar to the 5 step model I just rolled out in this chapter.

Step 1 – Bring order to the universe.
When you start, the clues look something like what's in the box: minute and fragmented. So – blow them up so you can see them, and sort them by general topic. Sifting and sorting is the essence of good detective work. But it's also as boring as watching the grass grow so they don't show it on the TV. You didn't appreciate it at the time, but I'd already done the heavy lifting for you on the first page of this chapter. I had already sifted and sorted the elements and clumped them into meaningful bunches (words). Without that, all you'd have had was a jumbled alphabet with no apparent meaning whatsoever.

DLAPXFA,JBKPEXIIOBXMQERKABO
XPTBABMBKALKKLKOBXPLKXYIBPFKP.

For all you know, the secrets of the universe – or utter nonsense - could be sitting right in front of you. Without the shifting and sorting, the same exact elements can take on entirely different meanings.

Step 2 – Start with the smallest unit of analysis.
The answer didn't lie in something as big as the corporate history of Church & Dwight Co., Inc. (that's who makes Arm & Hammer) or an analysis of the competing brands of baking soda. The answer lay in a much smaller unit of analysis - a single teaspoonful of soda. When they asked themselves what happened to a teaspoon of the stuff they found that the majority of it ended up in a batch of chocolate chip cookie dough.

Step 3 - Go with the obvious.
Who eats chocolate chip cookies? Mostly it's kids under 12. After the age of 12, consumption plummets as people get progressively concerned with zits and then weight as they

age. Who makes the cookies? Mom. It's an age old after-school ritual. Who buys the soda? Mom. She still does 70% of the grocery shopping, and 85% of the shopping for anything more than beer, milk, carbonated drinks and junk food. Most of the knowledge we need is common sense, and already stored in our brain.

Step 4 - Use what you know.
Arm & Hammer knew....

- More women were working - They weren't home to bake those after-school cookies - In fact, they weren't home to do a lot of things - Imagine the smell in their refrigerator, laundry hamper, rugs, etc.	- Mom needed Grandma's help - Grandma was stuffed in an old folks home, but her advice was still available -She used to have loads of old wive's remedies, like removing tea stains with baking soda -My mom wears tennis shoes
- each kids eats 17 cookies per week - There were fewer kids under 12 – so fewer cookies eaten - But cookies only use 1 lousy teaspoon of baking soda per batch anyway – who cares? - Is there any function that uses more than 1 tsp of soda at a time???	-Nobody was watching the kids -Working parents don't have time to really clean house -All they wanted was something quick & easy to mask the problems and clean up the obvious messes - They had lots of money to spend but no time

That's an odd array of information. In fact it's kind of like looking at

TEBK XII FP PXFA XKA ALKB, MOLDOBPP ABMBKAP LK QEB RKOBXPLKXYIB JXK.

It doesn't really make sense at first.

Step 5 - Use the context. Wait a minute. Let's use what we know. I see something! We're not getting beaten by a competitor. We're getting beat up by demographics. There are simply less potential cookie eaters out there and less moms to bake those cookies. No wonder we're taking it in the shorts. The first clue that cracks open a dilemma usually sits quietly in the middle of everything you already know. But you only find it if you take the time to formalize your intuitive knowledge.

Step 6 - Look for patterns. Let me see. There is a relationship or two in all the information. I can feel it. Let me study this for a minute ... I'll start by looking for repeated themes. No, they're not vowels, but repeated themes tell us the current situation. I see three distinct patterns: (1) Grandma and the importance of her old remedies; (2) both parents working, with no time for other responsibilities; and (3) the declining importance of kids. I got it! I know what to do. I just had an Adrian Monk moment.

Step 7 - Take the leap. The solution was clear. Arm & Hammer had to abandon its old market (juvenile cookie consumers) and go after a brand new market (working parents). And since baking soda can't make adults any smarter, or get them a job promotion, the only selling point left was to push the old wives remedies. So Arm & Hammer polled the collective grand parentage of its employees and found a ton of uses for baking soda around the house, including:

- ◆ as a medicine - for bee stings, sunburn and grease burns;
- ◆ as a non-abrasive cleaner - for teeth, china, pots & rugs;
- ◆ as a fire extinguisher - for grease fires;
- ◆ as a ph balancer- for stomachs, vaginas and pools;
- ◆ as an odor stopper - for under arms, refrigerators, ashtrays, drains and shoes.

This solution was a triple blessing: (1) they found a whole new market that had money to spend; (2) they found a lot more usage occasions for baking soda; and (3) on each usage occasion consumers would use a whole lot more soda than one lousy teaspoonful.

In fact, Mom would have to bake 6 batches of cookies every day for a month to use the same amount of baking soda it takes to deodorize the refrigerator. All Arm & Hammer needed was the courage to go ahead and take the leap. Much to their credit, they did. They advertised the old wives remedies with abandon, and the sales came rolling in. In fact, the response was so strong that they came out with their own formalized brands of toothpaste and personal hygiene products. Not too shabby. So, what do you think? Is the pattern technique useful at the practical level? Maybe just a tad.

A Closing Note

You've probably noticed that the pattern technique is the opposite of some other models, such as the Abstract Vault and Allegory models. They told you to start at the abstract level and then work your way toward specific details. This one tells you to start with the most specific of details (a single letter) then expand to the general level (the entire message). It is, in fact, a contradiction. But don't let that confuse you. It's just a nice example of the fact that we trigger explosive thinking and solve problems from opposite directions. There is no single right answer or right approach. Just find something that works for you.

Oh, and one last thing. Now you know why Wheel of Fortune is such a popular TV game show. All those couch potatoes who veg out on it are actually feeding their brains a pretty healthy diet. I think my grandma, the clear headed one, would be a fanatic Wheel-watcher if she were here today. The other one? Well, she'd probably try to imitate the wheel itself. Lord, she was dingy.

End Note
Note something interesting. This business about the smallest unit of analysis and the perception of patterns? It's Aristotelian logic. Aha! You just got a classical education. Whatcha think about that?

10
LIFE ON A LEASH
(KEEPING YOUR BRAIN UNDER CONTROL)

At the beginning, 90% of your ideas will be lousy. Once you've become an international grand master of creativity, however, only 50% of your ideas will be stinkers. Bad ideas are a fact of life, so don't get depressed. Instead, learn to get cozy with bad ideas, and then figure out a way to deal with them. My own suggestion is twofold –

1. avoid them if you can, and
2. kill them when you must.

Avoiding Bad Ideas

There's a danger to learning about creativity. You can get so enthusiastic that you go into overkill mode, making your products, plans or ideas a whole lot more complex than they need to be. According to David Kelley, president of a

Silicon Valley design firm, this problem has been especially acute in electronics. As one expert pointed out, "The guys who are designing most of these complex technological products are such techies that they think it's natural for everyone to hold down four buttons and twiddle a knob at the same time. They're so out of touch that they can't believe anyone would have trouble doing it."[1] The problem is, that little oversight can have a terrible effect in the marketplace.

Back in 1980, Xerox created just such a disaster. It came out with the 8200 copier, which was a marvel of modern science. It was the most advanced machine available, packed with so much on-board computer intelligence that it did everything except mow the lawn. But it was so complex that very few people could figure out how to copy a single page on it. Previously loyal Xerox customers bailed out in droves and - adding insult to injury - turned to Japanese copiers because the machines were simpler to use.

Sadly, Xerox was not alone. In the race for technological superiority, many firms made their products so complex that only a handful of techno-wonks could use them. Things got so bad that Kenneth Olson, the president of Digital Equipment Corp, confessed to his stockholders that he couldn't even figure out how to heat a cup of coffee in the microwave his own company had made.[2]

Not surprisingly, "user friendly" became a hot term in the early 1990's. All it meant was common sense: make a product that the average Joe can operate without swearing at his wife. The core of practical creativity is the K.I.S.S. strategy.

KISS - Keep It Short and Simple.

Edison didn't actually make the first light bulb. He made the first <u>usable</u> light bulb, because it was cheap and simple to manufacture and use.

Henry Ford didn't make the first automobile. He made the first <u>practical</u> automobile, because it was simplicity itself. Uneducated workers could assemble it in vast quantities, and the average Joe could fix it in his garage.

It was the same with the telephone, the telegraph and the rest of the machines and ideas that put the icing on the Industrial Revolution.

Simplicity is the soul of successful breakthroughs and applications. As Daniel Ling of IBM said, **"complexity is actually a sign of technological immaturity"**.[3] If you're just learning to express your own creativity, complexity is a trap you'll probably fall into now and then. So don't get discouraged. It's just that your creative faculty is immature, regardless of how sophisticated and mature you are in every other respect. Just learn to look at every idea and ask if it's as simple as possible, because simplicity can be a major competitive edge. A case in point is the sound system market, where American upstarts are altering the nature of the industry.

Simple Sound

When the Japanese obliterated the American sound system industry in the 1970's, they did so with high-tech machines based on solid state computer technology. Customers could use them to pre-plan everything but the laundry. Programming replaced music as the major selling point, with systems having up to 50 buttons and an endless array of possible functions. Consumers caught the high-tech bug, and according to one industry expert, "[the Japanese] brainwashed Americans into thinking more is better, that lights and buttons were more important than playing music."[4] Within a decade the Japanese literally wiped out the U.S. competition, and by the mid 1980's it was difficult to even find an American manufacturer.

Does this sound like I'm contradicting myself? After all, I just got finished anointing simplicity as the route to success. Now I'm showing the Japanese triumphing with rabid complexity. What gives? Just this - there's a big difference between short term and long term success. Bells and whistles always get attention in the short run. But in the long run, consumers actually do a pretty good job of gravitating toward the important features.

This can be illustrated by the fact that the surviving American audio executives stumbled upon the allegory that "listening to your stereo is like going to a concert". Once they bought into that image they realized something so obvious it's absurd. Not only did they discover the notion of wrap-around sound, but they also realized that folks don't get dressed in tuxes and formals so that they can sit in a little room and play with knobs. Then this common sense was reinforced by a little marketing research: consumers couldn't figure out how to run their high tech sound machines, and the thought of wading through encyclopedic instruction manuals just to listen to one song had lost its charm. In short, Japanese sound executives didn't have the good sense possessed by the Japanese copier manufacturers. And that told the American executives something _very_ important - the Japanese are not invincible. They're just good.

These realizations fueled the phoenix-like resurrection of the American sound industry, based on two simple assumptions: first, the purpose of a sound system is to produce sound;

second, you shouldn't have to be a computer programmer to get it to work. The Americans attacked the Japanese at all levels.

> In the high-end market Sound by Singer, from New York, came out with a $150,000 audio system that had only 3 controls: volume, balance and selection. It took only 30 seconds to master the entire system, and it produced incredible sound.
>
> In the mid-range market, Madrigal Audio Laboratories Inc., of Middletown, Connecticut produced a $2,150 system called the "Proceed PCD 2" which had only 5 controls: play, stop, pause, preview and advance. It also violated the Japanese standard of a low sleek horizontal cabinet. It was a boxy upright, which meant the user didn't have to go through squat torture to see the buttons ... and it also produced excellent sound.
>
> And at the low end of the market, the NAD 5325 player (out of Boston) was equally simple, sold for $300 ... and produced excellent sound.

The American companies put their money into making better sound rather than into making better buttons. Simplicity prevailed as they reintroduced the market to user-friendly sound. And here's the real joy - by 1991, 60% of the high-end audio equipment built in the U.S. was exported to Japan. En garde, mon ami! We will eat your ears.

Look at the Peanut, George

When George Washington Carver was a boy he dreamed of doing great and marvelous things. Then one night, according to Carver, God paid him a visit and said "George, don't aim so high. You can't handle anything larger than a peanut". So Carver took the Almighty at His word and put all his energy into the lowly peanut. As a result, he revolutionized the way the world looks at agricultural products. He opened the door to their use as fuels, medicines, lubricants and industrial raw material. He turned the world on its ear, by simply focusing on a little ole goober.

It takes as much creativity to rework a peanut as it does to discover nuclear fusion and the relative impact of the two can be about the same. So don't let "importance" tie you in knots. Twenty years ago, Pampers (Proctor and Gamble's famous diaper) was in a neck and neck competition with half a dozen manufacturers for the loyalty of America's little rosy bottoms. While its competitors were struggling to do something big, like create a diaper stuffing that would convert urine to jet fuel, P&G did something small. They changed the tape on Pampers. In fact, the new tape was actually inferior to the old. So much so that it lacked permanency. You could actually remove the tape, readjust it and stick it back on, all without ripping the diaper lining. Pretty feeble ... until you remember that babies don't hold still. They squirm around so much that you always have to readjust the tape. The result? Pampers blew the competition out of the water. Within six months it controlled the lion's share of the market and most of its competitors had folded, or retreated to the lab until they also came out with adjustable tape.

So what should _you_ do? Kiss your idea. Or should I say K.I.S.S. it --- keep it short and simple. And the best way to do that is often death. In short, you better know how to kill those bad (usually complex) ideas before they tie you in knots.

Killing Bad Ideas

After spending so much time talking about getting ideas, it may seem odd to talk about getting rid of them. However, it's just as important, and often harder to do. It's important because the vast majority of the ideas that come to mind aren't much good. But it's difficult to do because we work so hard to get an idea that we're reluctant to let it go.

The waste basket's your friend

In what seems like the distant past, I financed my way through grad school as a cartoonist. That sounds like such a quick and easy way to make money; but it was wrenching. I'd work for hours on one sketch - erasing, altering, adding, removing, and redrawing - never willing to give up on any idea until I had beaten it into submission. I made enough to pay the bills, but never moved beyond the point of doing toss-away art for training manuals. Meanwhile Steve Elde, a college buddy, had landed a job as the editorial cartoonist for Seattle's major paper.

My envy was mixed with the need to discover his secret, so the next time he came to town I invited him to a cartoon party. He accepted, on condition that he could assign the task. We sat down side by side working toward the goal of drawing an Indian that would make the viewer laugh, without the use of a written gag line. Steve was nerve wracking to work around. He sputtered, he laughed, and he ripped paper repeatedly. When we finished, my drawing sat on the same page I had originally touched. His sat on about the 30th, with the rest ripped and piled in the trash can. My drawing was cute. His gave you laugh-spasms. At that point he told me the secret of cartooning ... the trash can is your most important tool, not your pencil.

Instead of obsessively trying to fix a partially good idea, let it go, so that a better one can take its place. That's pretty frightening advice because most of us fear that idea #2 will never come. But have faith, there's more in you than you know.

I'm a case in point. I learned to throw away a lot of work, and in the process I got good enough so that my editor let me do the cartoons for this book. So now I'm a published artist.

Remote Control

The wastebasket works just fine if motivation is the only roadblock to dropping an idea. But sometimes you just can't get a bad idea out of your head even when you want to. It's like a scrambled satellite signal on TV; every time a new picture starts to come into focus, the old one comes roaring back to obliterate it. So what do you do? Try going with the TV analogy. Let your brain be the screen and your nose, the on/off button. Push it. It's pretty silly, but it often works. A variation is to imagine that your kids are watching trashy TV in the other room. Simply shout, "Turn that thing off!" It's even sillier than pushing your nose and a whole lot noisier. But it works pretty well, if you're not sitting next to a diamond cutter. If you are, you may want to try some quieter options.[5]

Diversions

If you wake up with a nightmare, you usually try to think about something more pleasant as you tentatively drift back to sleep. You're purposely creating a diversion. The same strategy can work when you're wide-awake. Simply think about something else totally unrelated. Think about fishing, fantasize about singing opera, or reminisce about your first date with so and so.

If that doesn't work, more drastic measures are needed. Change your scenery, go for a walk, or change your task. What the heck, go out and cut the grass. Primal urges are also a good distraction, which is why creatives are voracious consumers of food, spirits, sex, exercise and debate. Or if you're a bit more sedentary, curl up with a book or magazine ... or watch TV. Distraction is its chief value.

Fantasy Exits

I used to have a recurring nightmare common to many parents - my son David was hit by a car. I would wake up in a cold sweat with a severe case of the shakes. Yet as soon as I put my head down the nightmare returned, no matter what else I tried to think of. After several sleepless nights, I decided that the physician should heal himself. I disciplined myself to stick with the dream and shift it from reality to fantasy. David would still get hit, but he'd instantly turn into Mighty Mouse, complete with the ears and screwy looking tights. But he was so muscle-bound that he actually needed the auto-impact to achieve liftoff. So every time he got hit, the Mighty Mouse theme song would swell in the background and Mighty Dave would say "Thanks little buddy. I needed that." Eventually the dream got so silly it ceased to be a nightmare. Then it stopped altogether and I haven't had it for a couple of years now.

Weird? Yes. Silly? Of course. That's why they call it fantasy. The point is that a fantasy exit can work wonders.

> Let's say you come up with a promotional idea for your shoe store. You'll give a Baby Ruth to every kid who walks in the door. After a moment of reflection, though, you realize that your location near the mall's centerpiece fountain spells disaster. You won't sell a single extra shoe. All you'll do is feed the teenagers that hang around

all day making eyes at each other, and they'll chase away the paying customers. You need another idea. But every time you try, the teenagers re-occupy your mind: they sit on the counters; lounge on the chairs; beg for seconds; and chase away that blue-haired lady who will buy twelve pairs of shoes in a single sitting.

If you want to lose those brain suckers, shift into fantasy mode. Don't run away from the troublesome thought. Make the troublesome thought so bizarre that it dies from its own weight of absurdity. Puberty invades the store. You immediately cork every mouth with a candy bar, and while they gag on the paper you steal Daddy's' credit cards and ring up a $300 bill on each and every one of them. The cops come and throw you in the slammer for 20 years. As you shuffle around the exercise yard one day you realize that you're in the middle of a gold mine; and upon your eventual release, you sew up the shoe concession for the state prison system. You become a multi-millionaire and get your picture on the cover of Business Week.

Yoo hoo. They're gone, aren't they. The teenagers. You stopped thinking about them when the cops hauled you away. And you also came up with an idea you can pursue without going to jail. That's killing an idea with flare.

Brain Shift

So far we've been getting rid of ideas by running to neutral ground. But you can also try a more aggressive route which involves forcing the next idea in line to take its place. This technique grows out of the assumption that the different hemisphere's of the brain house different mental functions; one side handling abstract conceptual material, and the other side handling the compulsive details. What you try to do is perform shock therapy without the electrodes. You force your attention to jump to the unused hemisphere, or jump back and forth between the two. But how do you do that without leaving burn marks on your temples?

One method involves oxygen deprivation. Quick, stick a finger up your nose. (This assumes you're reading in private). Now remove the finger and insert it in the other nostril. Could you breathe through each nostril equally as well? Usually not. The assumption is that the open nostril is either the cause or result of focusing on one side of the brain. So here's what you do - block the clear nostril and force the clogged one to keep you from suffocating. It supposedly shifts the unused brain hemisphere into gear. If nothing else, it makes you stand out in a crowd.

A somewhat more sedate approach involves paper and pencil exercises. Do a crossword puzzle, or make up a math problem and solve it. They'll take you to the detail-oriented hemisphere. Or doodle; draw cartoons, boxes, arrows daggers etc. That takes you to the abstract side. Or do both, and bounce back and forth between the lobes until something gives. If that doesn't do the trick, work the crossword puzzle with one hand while doodling with the other. That wakes the whole cranium.

And as a last ditch effort, write a memo to yourself with your "off" hand. If you're right handed, take a pencil in your left and write "I hate mental blocks. They frustrate the heck out of me and I feel stupid trying these silly stunts." By this point your brain won't know which lobe is which. If you still can't get rid of the old idea, return to the diversion mode and take a nap. Or go kill a horse.

Killing the horse

If you ever capsize in a rapid river, never try to swim directly across the current toward shore. Your aggressive exertions will only wear you out and you'll drown. Instead, let the current carry you downstream, and swim diagonally to it, making slow progress toward the river bank. You may travel a mile or so downstream before you reach dry land, but that sure beats kissing the bottom. The same strategy can work on a bad idea. Sometimes it's so strong that fighting it directly is counterproductive. So instead of fighting it, use its strength to help yourself get out. Here's an example: you need an idea for selling women's shoes, and you figure motion is a good selling point.

You conjure the image of a horse. A grand white stallion, galloping through a forest with a beautiful woman on its back. You watch it run. You glory in its strength. You marvel at its grace. She ain't bad, either. On and on it runs; the dappled sunlight, the rhythmic pounding, the sense that earth and horse are one. Then you realize it's a loser. It goes nowhere. It doesn't sell the shoe. You need another idea. But every time you try, that darn horse comes galloping back.

Relax. Don't panic. Don't try to escape. In fact, go back to the horse scene and let it carry you along. All you have to do is one little thing. Shoot the horse. Crash, tumble, screams. Quick. Who shot the horse? There's a crossbow behind that tree over there. A figure emerges from the shadow. It's a king, or a baron, or some such princely guy. And he's not bad looking. In fact, he looks a little like Errol Flynn. He glides over, scoops up the lass and carries her lovingly to his palace. He washes her and tends a minor bump on her head. They talk. Eyes glisten with expectation. He feeds her a private banquet. We watch their hands fondle a goblet. Then he dresses her in regal robes. When he gets to the shoes, they fit perfectly and he marries her on the spot. My god, this is Cinderella, not Nanook, queen of the Amazons! And you just shifted your attention from motion to relationships as the major selling point. You also forgot about the horse, didn't you?

A final word on idea execution

Our peek at execution techniques is just that, a peek. It is not the end all and be all of knowledge, just something to whet the appetite. But frankly, it sounds kind of fun. It might be worth having a bad idea, just to go through the exercise of killing it.

End Notes

1. Bruce Nussbaum and Robert Neff, "I Can't Work This Thing!", <u>Business Week</u>, April 29, 1991, p. 60

2. Bruce Nussbaum and Robert Neff, "I Can't Work This Thing!", <u>Business Week</u>, April 29, 1991, p. 60

3. Bruce Nussbaum and Robert Neff, "I Can't Work This Thing!", <u>Business Week</u>, April 29, 1991, p. 60

4. Andrew Singer, quoted by Bruce Nussbaum in "High End Stereo: Simplicity for a Price", <u>Business Week</u>, April 29, 1991, p.62.

5. Shared with the author by his wife. It works, but it's less painful to kill a horse.

11
DOCTOR! DOCTOR!
(CURING MENTAL BLOCK)

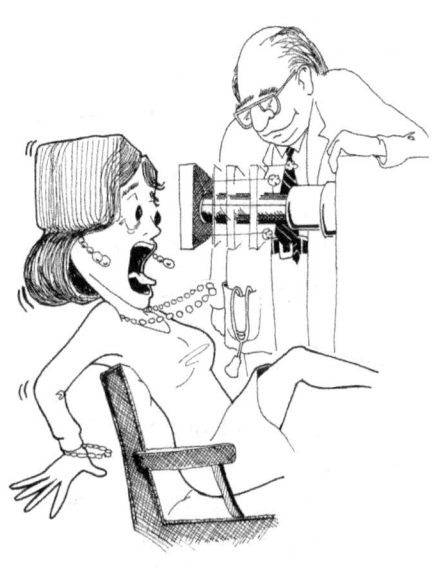

General Douglas MacArthur is justifiably listed among the bravest and most creative of all America's military commanders. As a Captain during the 1914 Mexican campaign he'd made a daring one-man raid behind enemy lines to capture three train engines for American use. During World War I he served as Chief of Staff for the American contingent and still insisted on being at the front, where he led numerous attacks, won nine decorations for heroism and was promoted to General in command of the Rainbow Division. During World War II his Pacific offensive became the benchmark of creative excellence in amphibious warfare, and his invasion of Inchon during the Korean War is still considered one of the boldest master strokes in the history of military strategy.

And yet, during one fateful period of his life, Douglas MacArthur suffered from a mental block that caused disastrous results. Pearl Harbor was attacked at 2:00 a.m., Philippines' time. Upon notification of that event at 3:00 a.m., MacArthur sat down to read his Bible. The Japanese finally got around to mounting an air raid on the Philippines nine hours later and, much to their surprise, found that MacArthur had done nothing to mount a defense. The last planes in the Pacific Air Force were still on the ground, and the majority of the remaining American fleet was still anchored close together in Manila Bay. They were destroyed in place without making even a token resistance.

But the worst was yet to come. MacArthur knew that the next step was a Japanese invasion. He also knew that his only hope was to retreat and outlast a siege of the Bataan Peninsula and Corregidor Island. Yet, MacArthur made no move to stock them with supplies, despite the fact that a nearby depot held enough food and ammunition to support his troops for four years; and despite the fact that the Japanese waited two whole weeks before mounting their attack. Instead, MacArthur spent most of his time methodically sticking colored pins in a map, but failing to issue any orders. As a result, America's military genius doomed his troops and prolonged the war for several needless years.[1] .. <u>That</u>, my friends, is mental block.

We've just cruised through five chapters of creativity techniques, with over thee dozen tactics. And you know something? It's entirely possible that none of them will work, for you. You stare at them. You memorize them. You even copy them and paste them on the wall. Like MacArthur, you come up with nothing, zero, zilch. What's going on? You've got mental block.

Take a look at someone who's struggling to be creative.
- ◆ They rub their eyes a lot.
- ◆ They wipe them.
- ◆ They massage them.
- ◆ And sometimes they dig at them to the point of gouging them out.

That's because mental block manifests itself as a solid wall of fuzz that stands right against your nose and prevents you from seeing what's on the other side. Vague shapes may appear now and then, but nothing comes into focus. And that "almost" quality is the most frustrating part about it.

Another frustration is that mental block even prevents you from using the very techniques which are specifically designed to help you get started. You can flip through the pages of this book. You can read the words and diagrams. But you can't really see them, or what lies within them. There's just this mental fuzz everywhere you look. When a blind man can't even find his cane, things can get a little tense.

Therein lies the trap, because tension is the cause of mental block in the first place. Stress shuts down our normal abilities to think because it triggers adrenalin overload that over-focuses our attention on picayune details and disconnects our ability to see anything beyond the end of our nose. This is the second major reason why relaxation is a key to creativity.
- ◆ The first, as you'll remember, was that it unlocked explosive thinking.
- ◆ This second reason is that relaxation prevents that self-defeating adrenalin overload we call mental block.

Don't let stress get the upper hand. Unless you have a rare talent, it's tough to be desperate and relaxed at the same time. So instead of trying to force your way blindly through the block, why not step back and borrow some wisdom from the psychologists and novelists? They have a few mental health tricks that can be very useful.

The first and foremost is to keep things in perspective. No matter how grim the problem, most of us will never have to contend with the life and death decisions that short-circuited the General. When you look at it that way, any other problem you face is pretty small potatoes. So realize the true proportions of your situation and turn down the adrenalin a notch, okay. Once you do that, I've got 29 little gimmicks that can help you through all sorts of mental blocks.

The Fear of Incompetence

Sometimes the task itself simply stresses you out, even when there's no specific danger attached to it. When that happens, sit down and list the reasons you can't get creative. That part's pretty easy, because there's a chronic whiner trapped in all of us. Two of the things you may discover are: (a) that your standards are too high (this thing has to be perfect); or (b) that your self esteem is too low (I just don't know enough to pull this off). No wonder you're stressed! You feel incompetent. But that sense of incompetence is curable. All you have to realize is that competence is nothing more than the balance between the requirements of the task and your capabilities. To bring things back into balance, all you have to do is lower the requirements and/or raise your capabilities.

Lowering the Apparent Requirements

1. **Write "<u>I don't have to outrun the bear</u>"** on an index card and tape it someplace that's constantly in view.

Remember that story? It meant that you don't have to be perfect. In fact, there isn't a task in the world that has to be done perfectly. The proof? You and me. If God is the all time creativity champ, and he made us - that's proof positive that perfection isn't a requirement. So lighten up.

2. **<u>Bite off small pieces</u>**. Every task is a combination of sub-tasks. When you look at them all as a complete set, they can be overwhelming. So don't look at them as a complete set. See how easy this is? Break the task into its component parts and just focus on one thing at a time.

3. **<u>Do the easiest sub-tasks first</u>**. Don't worry about flying right off the bat. Worry about putting on those silly tights. Then worry about finding a phone booth. By the time you've conquered all the easy steps your confidence will be ready for the tough part ... kissing Lois Lane.

4. **<u>Reward yourself along the way</u>**. Keep a drawer full of "hero of the revolution" buttons and slap one on your chest each time you succeed at a sub-task (Wow! I got out of bed). It's a technique that's kept Communist China rolling along for 50 years. It might work well for you too, Comrade. Or, if you're a capitalist at heart, give yourself material rewards: food, sex, a shopping spree, etc. One executive I know keeps a jar on his desk labeled "TIPS", and puts a buck in the jar every time he finishes a sub-task.

5. **<u>Get silly</u>**. Nothing deflates sanctity like the needle of irreverence. It puts the task into perspective. Jesse Jackson joked about New York being "Hymmie Town" while he was laboring mightily to put together his rainbow coalition. Morticians joke about the absurdities of rigor mortis. Every nurse has a funny story about bed

pans and catheters. And nuclear scientists cook hot dogs in the reactor at odd moments.

6. **Declare that your efforts are an experiment**, not a real solution. Nothing frees you up like a lack of accountability.
7. **Put someone else's name on the project, proposal or report**. It frees you up to be a ghost writer or anonymous genius. And if you're really perverse, use the name of someone you don't like. That way, you get the delicious fantasy of their demise if your work is lousy.

Raising Your Apparent Capabilities

8. **You know, you're not really by yourself**. You can always *ask someone for advice*, information and tips. Tom Edison, you will recall, spent a lot of time chatting with Professor Henry Rowland. I'd say that advice raised Edison's capabilities. What do you say?

9. **Look downhill**. If life is like climbing a mountain, most of us use each conquered peak as a vantage point to see how much farther we have to climb. Well smarten up and look the other way. Look back down the mountain, and see how far you've come. Pat yourself on the back now and then.

10. **Surround yourself with trophies**. That "Boy of the Year" citation from 8th grade is important. It's tangible proof of who and what you are. So is your bowling trophy. Fill your work space with all the tangible proofs of your greatness. Who cares if it impresses visitors? Let it impress the hell out of *you*.

11. **Catalog your expertise**. Sure, list all the degrees and certificates; but also list every talent and hobby. Then list all the things you've gained from your personal experience, bedtime reading, TV viewing and observation of everyday life. By the time you start your second ream of paper, you'll realize you've got more to offer than you thought.

Re-Discovering Creativity

The fear of incompetence is not the only problem. Sometimes we simply forget what creativity feels like.

12. **Reminisce**. Talk to someone about a great creative idea or venture in the past. Regale each other with tales and rehash what made it great ... and listen to the conversation. You'll be listing the key ingredients.

13. **Reporting**. Describe the process you went through when you were humming along on a successful creative venture. What was the problem? How did you crack the case? What did it feel like? What went through your mind? Why aren't you writing this down? It's your blue print.

14. **Reverberation**. Get a sounding board. I used to run a church camp, where the chaplain had the kids for an hour each day. Imagine, if you will, the difficulty of entrancing them with religion while they'd rather be sailing. Now that's a creative challenge! So every night Denny Moon, the chaplain, visited my cabin with a pained expression and the claim of mental block. I'd toss him a coke and ask him what his topic was. He'd tell me. I'd feed him some Oreos and ask him what he wanted to accomplish on that topic. He'd tell me. We'd toss some darts and I'd ask him what the best way to fulfill his goal was. And he'd run out of the cabin

chanting "I got it! I got it!". He was a brilliant and creative chaplain. And whether he realized it or not, he exploited me all summer long. I was nothing more than his sounding board. Einstein could have used my company.

Dealing with Inertia

Sometimes the fuzz comes from inertia. Creativity is hard work and sometimes the brain would rather stay in bed. So you have to jump start it with mental calisthenics.

15. **Beethoven's Bane**. Ludwig had a perverse neighbor. He'd wait until Beethoven was asleep then sneak over to his piano and play an arpeggio, up and down the octave ... except he'd omit the last note. Ludwig would have to haul himself out of bed swearing like a plumber, trot down to his own piano and hit the last note, just so he could go back to sleep. Do the same thing to yourself. Never stop a day's work at a natural breaking point. Always write the first sentence of the next section. Or better still, just half of a sentence. It'll force you into high gear first thing in the morning, and then you'll be back in full swing.

16. **Blitzkrieg**. If your project is sculpture - make gravel. If it's visual - scribble. If it's written - speed write. Don't even focus on doing the task right or accomplishing anything. Just do the mechanics of the task as fast and furious as possible. Your brain will take a break and adrenalin will take over. After that you'll be in high gear.

When I was in college I took a figure drawing class. One night the professor brought in the most beautiful model I had ever seen. She undraped, and her naked body was the kind of temple one wished to worship for hours on end. But that

SOB of a professor made us do a series of 30-second quick sketches. I didn't have time to worship. I just drew like a banshee. After 10 quick poses, he excused that model, and my heart along with her. Then he brought in a model that was, well frankly, she was fat and ugly. "Now" he said, "take an hour on this one". You know something? I was so obsessed with the need to observe that I found a beauty in her which I would never have seen otherwise. The result was the best nude I'd ever drawn. That professor was pretty clever. That one night is one of the things that led me to this book

The Lack of a Hook

Our creativity doesn't do a thing for mankind. It has no direct effect on IBM, our family or any other abstract entity. But ... our creativity does have a very real impact on the real live individuals who make up mankind, IBM and families around the world. When we forget that other **people** are the ultimate target of our efforts, the fuzz can set in. So make your creativity very personal.

17. **Aim your solution at a specific person**. Put their picture on the wall, even if it's just a magazine picture of someone like them. Refer to them by name and include all the personal comments you'd make to them face to face. They can be edited out later.

18. **Write a letter to a specific (real or imagined) friend**; or use your Mom or dead grandfather if you wish. Tell them what the problem is and why you can't get creative about it. Tell them why you wish you could be creative and list all the wonderful things your creativity would do for them. Sometime before you write your final farewell, you'll be surprised to find that you've been generating a fair amount of useful creativity. Transfer the ideas and trash the letter. You're in gear.

Change and Stimulus

Sometimes, a change of pace may be all you need.

19. **Change tools.** Draw with the eraser instead of the lead. Use a pen instead of a pencil. Use your PC instead of a pencil. Turn off the PC and use lipstick instead. Or forget about writing instruments and use a tape recorder. Or try shock therapy, use a video camera.

20. **Change surfaces.** Use lined paper instead of unlined, or vice versa. Turn the paper sideways. Write on index cards instead of paper. Write on the wall. Better still, go to a bar and write on cocktail napkins.

21. **Change positions.** Stand instead of sit. Hemingway wrote on the top of his dresser, and Thomas Jefferson always read standing up. Sit instead of stand, or lay down to work. Abe Lincoln stretched out in front of a fire whenever he had something important to do. Poets are notorious for composing their verse in bed. And the McDonalds headquarters building has a circular water bed reserved for folks who need to think great thoughts. Or if you tend to sit on a foot, switch feet.

22. **Change your regimen.** Take the bus to work instead of the car. Eat your dessert first. Put your shoes on before your socks. Whatever. Just break your pattern a little and your brain will see things a little differently.

23. **Change clothes.** Aside from improving the fragrance of the room, it may also benefit your mind. Some people are strongly affected by what they wear and can manage their mood by the color and texture of their clothes. Sunny colors and smooth fabrics make them upbeat or romantic. Dark colors or bulky fabrics make them

serious and ponderous. The old stereotype about women buying hats and underwear to manage their moods seems to hold true as well. In addition, clothes include costumes, which seem to work well for some people - especially if they're role playing.

24. Take a shower. There's a rhythm to the water that speaks to the mind as well as the body. There's a cleansing effect that tends to wash away stress and bring relaxation. Also, there's something primal about getting naked, especially at 2:00 in the afternoon. It's the ultimate change of clothes. As a fall back, if you're fuzzed-out in public, wash your face. It's not quite as good, but it keeps you out of jail.

25. Change your environment. Work in the hall instead of your office. Switch desks with your secretary. Work in a storeroom, or set up shop in your local public library. Turn on the radio if you prefer silence, and turn it off if silence is your enemy. Or sleep during the day and work at night.

26. Change your privacy quotient If you usually labor in private, go grab someone for an audience. Or work in the midst of a noisy crowd. Come to think of it, why not go whole hog and set a table out on the sidewalk? And if you're a chatty little somebody who sits in the midst of a bull pen; stuff cotton in your ears, put on a hat with a long bill, and put a sign on your desk that reads, "DO NOT DISTURB! BRAIN AT WORK."

There's a State Department official I know who does her best work by going native, sitting topless in the city park during the lunch hour. Now there's a change in privacy. Of course, she's stationed in Rio de Janeiro. It might not work as well in Chicago.

27. Take an external break. Crawl out of your head and go shoot some hoops. Visit a museum. Catch a movie or just simply visit with someone. When you neglect such breaks, it means you think the task is a life or death matter. And when you elevate it to that level you climb right back into the competency trap with which we started. The requirements of the task will seem a whole lot bigger than your capabilities. Then you'll have to go through this entire list all over again.

28. Shift into neutral and take an internal break. Be still and silent. Get away from all noise makers and external stimuli, and draw into yourself. Meditation is good. So are self- hypnosis or bio-feedback techniques. And to tell you the truth, so is a good old fashioned nap. When you can hear your heart beat, and the soft rhythm of your own breathing, you will have arrived at the quiet center of the internal you.

29. Pray. I realize that I jeopardize my image as a two-fisted, worldly kind of guy with this one. But I stand by it. Prayer is a marvelous tool. On the one hand, I believe there is a God, and that He sometimes answers prayer. On the other hand, even if I'm wrong, the act of prayer is incredibly healthy.

- ♦ It makes you feel like you're not alone. That can be very comforting when you've vaulted the wall and stand out there in the meadow all by yourself.
- ♦ In addition, the act of stating your needs to another party can help you see what your real problem is.
- ♦ And since prayer is the only truly private conversation we ever have, we tend to be more honest there than anywhere else.

♦ Finally, prayer gives your brain a break. It is literally a different activity than trying to figure out a new design for your product.

So if the notion of God gives you a problem, try praying to a kumquat or an old vase. Who knows? It might work as well.

Farewell to Mental Blocks

There you have it. If you have a mental block, I have the solution. Somewhere in the preceding list you'll find the intellectual plunger that will clear things out for you. Either that or the preceding list will remind you of a technique that worked for you as a kid. And since creativity is in many respects a child-like pursuit, always go back to what worked as a kid.

Chocolate chip cookies did the trick for me. It calmed me right down, because it let me know that Mom was in her kitchen and all was right with the world. Twenty years later I figured the same thing would work for others, so I spent 10 years inviting my MBA students over to my home once a week for an open house. I'd toss a log in the fireplace and set out a plate of fresh baked chocolate chip cookies. And the future leaders of America sat around like true floor-dwelling creatures and basked in the momentary safety of childhood. They were also incredibly creative in class and I look forward to great things from them in the future

You see, creativity is more a state of mind than a collection of techniques, tricks and gimmicks. In the final analysis, everything in this book is a crutch. Very useful, but not always necessary. If your state of mind is on target, you'll shift into high gear without consciously using any of this.

Of course, it's a comfort to know that if you start to sputter, you've got a resource like this sitting on the book shelf.

We have now come to the end of the real nuts and bolts section of this book on creativity in the trenches. We've looked at an arsenal of weapons, and how to use them. From the incredibly simple to the mind-bendingly complex, you my friend are now educated. Just one more little issue. You could go nuts in the process. Why don't we take a look at that in our next chapter?

End Note
1. William Manchester, <u>American Caesar</u>, Boston, Little Brown and Company, 1978, pp. 205-220

12
STANDING IN THE COW PIES
(STRUCTURE)

Congratulations! You're over the wall. You've been inspired. You've gained courage. You've got a tool chest full of techniques and the willingness to soar. So you've vaulted the wall, and now you stand out in the meadow .... with your foot firmly planted in a cow pie. In fact, both feet inhabit a cow pie, because that's all the meadow is ... an endless stretch of random ideas. But take heart. Since you were the cow that dropped all these meadow muffins, they won't kill you - but they will impede your progress unless you clean things up a bit. At a minimum you need a path.

The Need for Structure

Having ideas is only half the battle. **Doing** something with them is the other half. The world is full of brilliant losers, those people who are delightful company on a bar stool. They easily float over any wall, but haven't the faintest notion of what to do once they land in the meadow. Consequently, they have plenty of time on their hands, because no one has any use for their ideas. That's because they lack discipline and order. In short, they lack structure.

I've spent a lot of time extolling the virtues of intellectual and emotional freedom, in an attempt to help you defy gravity on your way over the wall. But there is an acute danger in that tactic. The danger is that you might get the message that anything that smacks of discipline and order (i.e. structure) is a violation of that freedom. So let me drop a quotable quote on you to clarify things:

> "Structure turns fantasy into creativity."

Structure gives us a foundation of premises, assumptions and facts. Without that solid footing, all we could do is flail away in random fashion. Structure also guides our search for ideas. Finally, structure tells us how to go about using those ideas. It gives us the rules of the road, and without it all we create is a mental traffic jam called "information overload". We short circuit, get a little goofy, and entertain strangers from our bar stools.

Structure and the Wall

Structure is what makes life inside the old wall so comfortable and productive. I know what you will do. You know what I will do. The two of us can therefore interact with a minimum of heated negotiation and frustration, and a maximum of effectiveness and efficiency.

There is a prescribed way to view life inside the wall. When your gut gets a knot, you know to interpret that as hunger.

There is a prescribed way to order activity. You know that hunger requires an orderly flow of activities: (a) you go to an appropriate retailer (a grocer rather than hardware store), (b) you serve yourself rather than waiting for an employee to run down the aisles getting your order, and (c) you pay for your food before you consume it.

There is a prescribed protocol for conducting affairs. You stand by the food conveyer belt and act grumpy, because you're the customer. I stand on the other side and add up the prices, acting like I'm really glad to deal with your grumpiness, because I'm wearing the uniform that says I'm a cashier.

There is a prescribed set of rewards and punishments which guide everyone's behavior. If the service is good, you'll tip me a quarter for carrying six 40 pound bags of groceries 220 yards through snow drifts. If the service is bad, you'll withhold the tip, complain to my boss and get me fired.

Life makes sense within the wall because each and every activity has its own prescribed structure. Consequently, I can predict what will happen, make plans, and act accordingly. And so can you.

What Happens When Structure Is Violated

If you have any doubt about the importance of structure, try this simple experiment --- switch the protocols for grocery stores and restaurants.

Wear a tux to the grocery store, perch on a stack of display items and snap your fingers until a stock boy comes by. Demand to be seated in the non-smoking area, then hand him your shopping list and complain about how slowly he brings everything back to you. Open every can and package on the spot. Sample a steak and send it back for being too rare. Heck, send it back for being completely uncooked. Then eat the rest. Keep pestering the stock boy for seconds on coffee. Ask for a doggie bag, then demand that the cashier come to you, instead of you waiting in the checkout line. Give her your Diner's Club card when she finally comes and have her remove the Del Monte green beans from the bill since they weren't spiced to your liking. And when the manager comes to evict you, tip him sweetly and mention that next time you'd like to sit closer to the orchestra.

As you rest up in your neighborhood jail, you can reflect on the fact that folks within the traditional wall take their structure very seriously. We know this because you've been charged with public nuisance, shoplifting, malicious mischief or worse ... for a behavior that would have been perfectly fine within the "proper" context.

Some of you will have seized on this scenario as a multi-million dollar brainstorm for a new grocery chain. If you are one of those people, go with my blessing, and send me 1% of your gross. For the rest of you, your response to the scenario is "of course". You know that society relies on a rigid structure for its smooth operation.

Structure and Wall Vaulting

When we vault the wall, we leave society behind. Consequently, the rules and structure that worked so well back within the old wall may be irrelevant. In fact, they may even be dead wrong. But most of us try to drag them out into the meadow with us anyway. When that happens we become our own worst enemy. Stop and think about that for a minute.

Just about everyone complains about grocery shopping. Either they think that groceries are too expensive or they moan about the hassle of finding a parking space and pushing a cart through miles of aisles, only to stand in the checkout line for an hour. Consequently, every grocery chain in America is trying to offer lower prices, more convenience, or both. Those organizations are trying to jump the wall, but most of them are trying to bring the old rules and structures along with them.

> Several grocery chains wanted to be the rock bottom grocer. So they held down costs by using part time help (no benefits) and placed inordinate performance demands on their employees. But their desire for tight fiscal control combined with their traditional image of what a grocery store should look and feel like, yielded a store that simply felt "cheap".

> In contrast, Walmart, Costco and Supermarche PA have changed the very nature of what cheap groceries mean. They don't even look like grocery stores. They look like warehouses. Their display areas have floor to ceiling cartons and crates. Elevator music, soft light and pristine fixtures are non-existent. And after the shopper takes a dolly rather than a shopping cart to the checkout line, they can use their credit card to pay for things.

On the other side of the fence, we have the grocery chains that are trying to stress quality and convenience. But they also suffer from trying to drag the same old rules and structures out into the meadow. They put carpeting in their wine department. They carry more competing brands. They put Victorian bric-a-brac on their shelves. And they have enough potted plants and brass railings to look like a fern-bar. But you still have to push a cart through endless aisles, and you still have to stand in the checkout line. It's still just a grocery store, in every sense of the word.

> A true jump outside this wall - complete with new rules and structures - is embodied by a few firms in Canada and California, who are turning grocery acquisition into a shop-at-home phenomena. With some, you order by phone. With others, you order using your personal computer. Then a delivery truck shows up within 4 hours and the stock boy literally stocks your pantry for you. Now that's convenience. Anything less looks like lip service.

> Even that pales in comparison to the true wall-vaulters that California breeds. Several inventive caterers have set up long term contract meal-plans for the two-income yuppies who want absolute convenience. Custom made breakfasts and dinners are delivered every day, hot and ready to eat.

Don't get me wrong. The cheaper grocery chains are doing pretty well for themselves. And so are the fern-bar grocery chains. It's just that they could be doing even better. Pulling the old rules and structures along with you may not kill you, but doing so can certainly hamper your progress.

The Dilemma

So we have a dilemma. We need structure. But we can't just carry the old structure with us. That means we need to generate our own. Or more precisely, **you** need to generate **your** own ... because mine won't do you any good. Well, it'll do you some good, but it's not divinely inspired.

The point is that vaulting the wall isn't an escape from structure. It's actually a conscious embrace of structure. You won't be able to take structure for granted anymore, or keep it at the subconscious level. You'll have to be the conscious creator and monitor of structure, all by yourself, because you are the only thing that stands between you and chaos. But before you get too worked up, let me assure you that generating a structure for yourself doesn't snuff your creative spark.

It doesn't violate the notion of freedom, because freedom actually means running easy in the harness. When you're out there in the meadow by yourself, it's a good idea to create your own anchor so that the winds of randomness don't blow you away. One of the nice things about standing out in the meadow to write this little book is that I get to make up my own rules and structures. One of those rules is that mixed metaphors are perfectly legitimate ... especially when they clarify my meaning. Harnesses and anchors go together quite nicely in this meadow. Structure doesn't violate the notion of relaxation either, because it establishes the predictability and certainty that help relaxation take root.

In fact, structure can actually stimulate the creative spark. Let's take this book as an example. First, assume that writing a book is a creative act. Second, let me be so bold as to suggest that things in this particular book are moving along pretty well to this point. So maybe we can agree that, yes, this project represents a fair bit of creativity. Then third, if you pause a moment, you'll realize that this book has been cramming structure down your throat from the very first page. I just have such a conversational tone that I can sneak it in on you relatively painlessly. If you'd like a little proof, let's do a quick review of how I wrote this book.

		Creativity		
		Innovation		
Creativity	Innovation	Paradigm	Innovation	Creativity
		Innovation		
		Creativity		

This book started with a clear definition of the creativity and how it differed from innovation, then it moved into the types of creativity and their applications.

	Invention	Synthesis	Modify
Idea			
Prototype			
Development			
Delivery			
Spinoffs			

We even delineated some of the bricks that make up the wall of rationality when we looked at the roadblocks, myths and observations about creativity.

Pride	Don't know Creativity	Don't want Creativity	Are not allowed it	Creativity & Nobility	
Pride	Missing Organ	Solitary Magician	The need For Genius	Risk	
	Necessity Is a Mom	Competitive Edge	Education Trap	Culture & Creativity	
Time	Teamwork's downside	Research Blinders	Efficiency vs. Effectiveness		

The structure of getting ideas. I also laid out a heavy dose of structure in Chapter 6 when we entered the "how to" phase of the book, starting with the section on linear and explosive thinking.

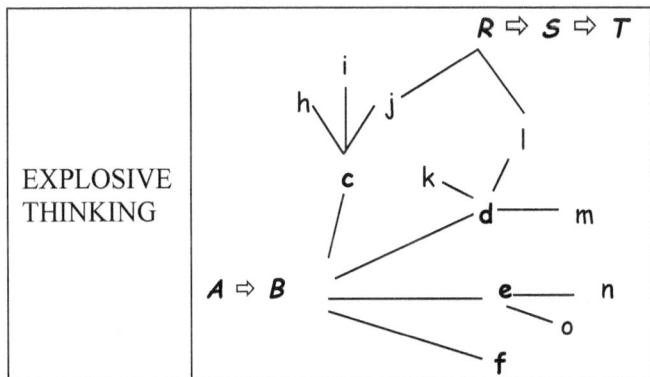

Next, we moved to the main model, the Opportunity Model, which told us where to look for ideas.

	Existing Situation	New Situation
Existing Tools	IMPROVE	PIONEER
New Tools	REDESIGN	DIVERSIFY

Then we looked at a very structured cookbook approach to specific old and new techniques for finding or generating ideas.

Allegorical Thinking	Abstract Vault	Historical Allegory
Problem Definition	Mind Mapping	Pattern Search	Reverse Logic
Vacuuming	**GETTING IDEAS**	Serendipity
Logical Extremes	Benefit Search	Plugging Away	Inside-out Thinking

We even went into considerable depth on the structural aspects of several techniques, such as Mind Mapping, and Imaging and Pattern Searches.

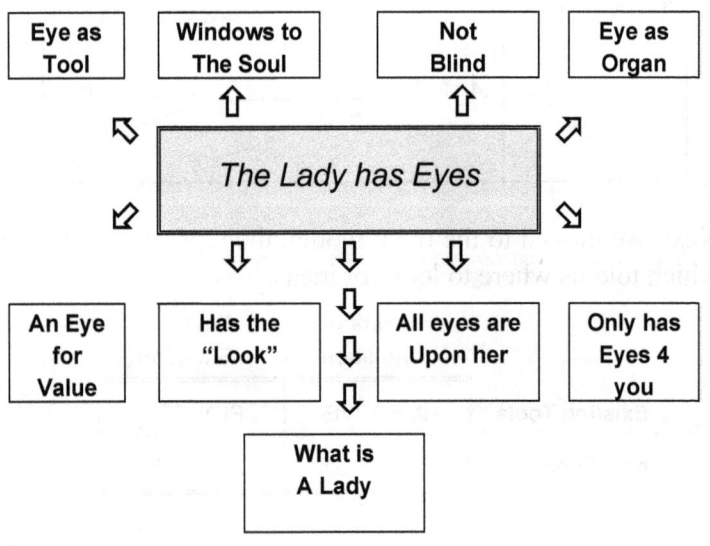

As you glaze over in realization of all the boxes and arrows I covered, take comfort from the fact that my wife just passed behind me and snorted "that stuff looks like electrical diagrams". She's absolutely right. I just wish she wouldn't snort,. Makes me want to duck and cover.

So ... Whadyathink?

This is what structure looks like. All those box and arrow wiring diagrams create a guard rail that keeps you on the road. Yet it needs to be broad enough to allow you to bounce around from lane to lane without going off the cliff. If you pause to recall all the subjective meanderings you've encountered within this book, I'd say that the structure has served us pretty well. And it's done so without being terribly obtrusive or restrictive.

So don't be put off by structure. It does not kill creativity. It just builds a corral around it so that you can go wild without hurting anyone, including yourself.

When you're out there in the meadow all by yourself, structure may be your best friend. Just remember that no one else can make the rules for you. So you better bring your own rules, or make them up on the spot. To help you out in that regard, the next chapter will suggest a number of ways to bring a little order and discipline to your work.

13
THE 6 EASY STEPS TO SUCCESS
(HOW TO STRUCTURE YOUR OWN CREATIVITY)

Some folks feel gypped if they don't walk away from a book with "The 6 Easy Steps to Success" in their hands. In fact, what they really want is: the 6 steps, the 5 traps, the 4 guidelines, the 3 pillars, the 2 choices and the 1 golden rule ... as though life could be run by simple equations.

If you're one of those people, I suggest you go watch the movie Jurassic Park. One of the main characters is Dr. Ian Malcolm, a mathematician who's big on Chaos Theory. Remember him? His point was that it's impossible to predict, plan or control the behavior of living beings using numbers, because living beings are too complex. Numbers, said Dr. Malcolm, are only good for predicting and controlling very simplistic things - such as nuclear reactions. Well, the folks at Jurassic Park ignored old Dr. Malcolm in the movie, and the result was mass mayhem and gore at the jaws of velociraptors and other hungry dinosaurs. There's a lesson in there somewhere, don't you think?

But how does that apply to us? Well people, it turns out, are every bit as intelligent and complex as dinosaurs. And when you put them into organizations, the complexity increases geometrically. So the "6 Easy Steps" approach to any human activity is absurd. But what the heck. The effort to reduce life to an understandable list is a noble pursuit. So I offer you my own 6 Easy Steps to structuring creativity – a complex expansion of the pattern search formula rolled out in the Dick Tracy chapter. I call it the COF-TOS system. It sounds like "cough-toss", which triggers the image of projectile vomiting. Now, try to get that image out of your head. I dare you. It's memorable.

Uncle Joe's 6 Easy Steps

1. **C**ollect information
2. **O**rder the information
3. **F**ocus on the key issues
4. **T**rigger ideas
5. **O**rder the ideas
6. **S**ell the Solution

Step 1 - Collect the Information

Fletcher Snively was a devout Christian living in Florida. Since he was experiencing financial difficulties, he earnestly prayed to win the state's $60 million lottery. The drawing came and went, and an agnostic in Sarasota ended up winning the pot. That evening, the Almighty visited Fletcher in a dream and Fletcher asked what happened. The Almighty smiled and said, "Fletcher, my son, you have to buy the ticket yourself."

Don't just sit around praying for a brainstorm. Divine revelation may work like a charm in the scriptures, movies and biographies, but my own experience is that the muses and the almighty don't come on command. So, the first step in the creative process is to get off your keister and do some legwork. Go out and get information, because making decisions in a vacuum sucks. Cruise the internet. Ask people – on or off line. Read a book. Plant yourself in the middle of the mall and study the people around you for 15 minutes. Now that Google and Wikipedia are firmly ensconced, there's not much of an excuse to be ignorant about anything.

The nice thing about gathering information is that it's often easier done than said. Yep, you read that right; easier done than said. That's because most of the information you'll need is already in your head. The problem is that we tend to ignore that vast storehouse of wisdom that resides between our own ears. So, let's eliminate that problem right now by summarizing the types of information you should gather.

FACTS. Those are the verifiable truisms about life that usually reside in the form of numbers and data: market share, advertising share, stock turnover, employee turnover, apple turnover, leverage ratios, interest rates, inflation rates etc., etc., ad nauseam (or ad cof-tos). These tidbits are a must, and the best way to get them is visit the vast libraries of the world online.

ASSUMPTIONS AND CLICHES.
- A penny saved is a penny earned.
- If some is good, more is better.
- When the going gets tough, the tough get going.
- If you need something done, ask a busy man to do it.
- If all you have is a hammer, everything looks like a nail.
- IBM has genetic myopia, every problem looks like an opportunity for main frame computers.

Clichés surround us. But we tend to forget that they got to be clichés for a reason. They represent assumptions and premises that seem to have some veracity. So make a list of your own assumptions and premises about the problem or opportunity you're trying to address. And don't forget your assumptions and premises about the other people and organizations that are key actors.
- Is price really the driving issue for customer A?
- What really motivates employee XYZ?
- What would your spouse really like for Christmas?

A little creative "assumptionizing" can unlock some very interesting insights.

STEREOTYPES. Men offer security to get sex, while women offer sex to get security. People don't just make up stereotypes. No matter what various advocacy groups say, stereotypes are based on observable fact. They're just not based on the total body of facts, that's all.

For instance, 23% of the female population really do want strangers to see them as objects of desire all the time (called sex objects). That's it – only 23%. But since that 23% likes to strut its spandex into every night club throughout the land, it's not surprising that some folks get the feeling that every woman must be like that. That's where the stereotype comes

from. It's absolutely true and accurate. It's just incomplete. The same is true of every other stereotype we have:
- ◆ blacks have natural rhythm,
- ◆ men have one-track minds,
- ◆ accountants are bean counters,
- ◆ playing in the rain will make you sick,
- ◆ investing in a bear market leads to ruin, etc, etc.

But the funny thing is that stereotypes don't need to be complete in order to be useful - due to something called the 80/20 principle - 20% of any population usually accounts for 80% of all the activity of that population in any given area. Everyone else kind of sits around like a lump. So while a stereotype won't be "true" in an absolute and universal sense, it sure will come in handy. My advice - make a list of your stereotypes about the people, organizations and situations you face. It makes a marvelous basis for decision making.

EXPERIENCES. What happened the last time you faced a situation similar to the one you find yourself in right now? The future will never be an exact repeat of the past, but it never hurts to see if you learned anything from the past. What happened? What should you have done? How did the winner get to be the winner? Write it down.

OBSERVATIONS. Stop thinking so hard and sit still. Now, look around you. What's going on? What's <u>not</u> going on. Who talks to whom? What do they say? What's important to them? What themes keep coming up? Who works with whom? Who loves/hates whom? How do people first react when they first see or hear about the issue you're trying to address? Americans drink less and less coffee each year, but we know that a human consumes the same amount of liquid year after year. So what are they drinking instead of coffee?

EXTRAPOLATIONS. Where does all this lead? If drinkers are substituting bottled water for coffee, will that pattern continue until 100% of all fluid needs are met, or will consumers finally realize that they can get the same thing out of their tap for 1% of the cost of bottled water? Remember designer jeans? They were hot until folks decided that the $30 extra was a bit much to pay for someone's autograph on their buns. No behavioral pattern ever goes to 100%. So you have to decide if the current situation is:
- a fad (very short lived); or
- a trend (medium lived); or
- a new order of being (longer lived).

Then you need to figure out what new product, activity or circumstances might bring an end to that fad, trend or order. Just to entertain yourself, look at the fads and trends in the sound industry.
- Thirty years ago, most music still came out on the old tried and true 33 rpm phonograph record.
- Then the 8-track tape hit the market, and phonograph records were obsolete.
- No sooner had the nation bought the bulky new tape players than the 8-track instantly died, with the advent of the cassette tape deck.
- Those, in turn, had a decade of success until they were replaced by the CD players and disks.
- Then CD's were attacked by DAT tapes and players.
- And then we got iPhones, and iPods and iRobots. So extrapolate your heart out. Where do you think things will be in 5 years?

DEDUCTIONS. If 40% of the adult population drinks three cups of coffee in the morning, and 52% of the adult population listens to at least 15 minutes of a morning radio talk show, what do you deduce? Aha! Maybe Chase and Sanborn should advertise on the morning talk shows! That act of synthesis is known as deductive reasoning. You take a number of bits of information, massage them together and generate a new bit of information.

GUESSES. There's absolutely nothing wrong with making a guess. Especially if you've played with the other forms of information first. Then you're making an "educated" guess. So record your guesses. They're bona fide information from a very reputable source ... you. And they're every bit as valid as the guesses that populate all the "hard" data you collected under our "facts" heading. Even something as supposedly factual as census data is loaded with guess work. Census takers don't actually count every nose. If someone's not home, they simply ask a neighbor. And if you've ever lived in an apartment house, you know that your guess of the number of inhabitants in the apartment down the hall is approximate at best.

FANTASIES.
- "Boy I'd like to make a million on this project."
- "Wow, I bet this stuff would make me popular."
- "If I wrote her a poem, she'd love me."
- "If we drop the price 10%, market share will grow 15%."
- "If I slipped on a negligee, he'd take out the garbage without complaining."
- "All I have to do is finish this book and I'll be creative."

Your life is filled with fantasies: secular and sacred; vocational and domestic; and sexual as well as functional. The same is also true for every other person. Consequently, acknowledging and unlocking those fantasies can give us a target for our creativity, show us the proper way to approach issues, and help us remove the obstacles that stand in our way.

Remember the myths about creativity back in Chapter 4 (the missing organ, the need for genius, the solitary magician etc)? Those were fantasies. The simple act of acknowledging them went a long way toward removing those obstacles and making us more creative. When it comes to other people, it can unlock opportunity ... like the fantasy that drinking coffee makes them grown up - along with smoking, drinking, wearing high heels and make up, getting their first driver's license, losing their virginity, buying their first home, having their first baby and ... wait a minute.

Did you ever notice something? Many of the fantasies we have involve the rights of passage; like the executive who confided to me that he finally felt like his father's equal (i.e. all grown up) the day he bought his first company.

A good fantasy check can be very useful. So make a list. What are the fantasies relative to the issue and/or people you're trying to address?

CONCLUSIONS. What do you think about all this? Or, what do you think about any of the individual facts, assumptions, stereotypes, experiences, observations, extrapolations, deductions, guesses and fantasies? What do you think about what you think? Should you write your thoughts down? Of course you should! They're "expert opinions", and that makes them valid information. Besides, if you don't write them down, you'll forget them, because creativity is a complex business. Okay. Take a break. Take a breath and look back at all the information you've just garnered. And realize that 9 of the 10 information sources we just covered are tucked away in your own cranium. You already have 90% of the information you'll ever need stuck between your ears. You just need to get it out on paper where you can see it.

Step 2 - Order the Information

The problem with collecting information is that you'll get so much of it, so quickly, that you'll create information overload for yourself. So you need a method for organizing all that info or you'll drown in your own brilliance.

Coffee is liquid brown mud	Brown is the color of Mother Earth	8% of pop. works with the soil	Outdoors makes us active & alive
Med. evidence: Caffeine is a simulant	Sales of Caff. Coffee are dropping	Coffee's taste is a problem for some folks	Stimulants make the heart beat Faster/harder
Sales of de-caf coffee are dropping	There are less coffee occasions	Sales of fruit juices are on the rise	Sales of soft drinks are steady
Brown = sin, dirty and evil to some	Most fiction covers good vs. evil	Men want a noble vocation	Don't have to work with soil to be noble
People sin because sin is fun	We love good vs. evil stories	Brown = sin, dirty and evil to some	Nothing beats coffee by a campfire
Health is a hot issue for consumers	Coffee is a grown-up's beverage	Coffee is under heavy scrutiny	Sales of bottled water are rising

There is no right way to do this, but let me suggest a three step approach that might be useful. Just don't treat it as gospel truth or you'll be jamming yourself inside someone else's wall. Feel free to use just one of the steps, or alter them. Or trash them and come up with your own. Remember, my job is to jog your brain, not control it.

BE A SCRIPT WRITER. Put each observation and bit of information on a separate index card. For clarity, you can use a different color card (or ink) for each type of information (assumption, fantasy, deduction etc). Or use a different color for each person involved, or for each aspect of the situation. Then lay all the cards out on the floor, pin them to the wall, or (if you're a hot shot with computer graphics) you can do the whole thing on your terminal.

		Outdoors makes us active & alive	Nothing beats coffee by a campfire
Coffee is liquid brown mud	Brown is the color of Mother Earth	8% of pop. works with the soil	Men want a noble vocation
	Brown = sin, dirty and evil to some	Good people drink coffee, not booze	Don't have to work with soil to be noble
	People sin because sin is fun	Most fiction covers good vs. evil	We love good vs. evil stories

****

		Coffee is a grown-up's beverage	Coffee's taste is a problem for some folks

****

Health is a hot issue for consumers	Medical evidence: Caffeine is a simulant	Stimulants make the heart beat faster/harder	Coffee is under heavy scrutiny

****

There are less coffee occasions	Overall coffee sales are dropping	Sales of "safe" liquids are up	Soft drink sales are steady

Script writers and novelists use this to find some pattern in all the odd bits of story lines, character traits and relationships they've been mulling over.

The next step is to read through the cards in some kind of order to see if a train of thought develops. "What order?" you ask. Well, here's where it gets interesting. Discipline yourself to read it in a number of orders.
- ◆ Start by reading the rows left to right.
- ◆ Then do it right to left.
- ◆ Then bottom to top, and vice versa.
- ◆ Then do it by column, up to down, then down to up.
- ◆ Then read it diagonally.

Whatever. The point is that you want to establish reading rules for yourself. They prevent you from trying to scan the whole array of information and thereby glazing into zombie land. The reading rules also force you to confront the information in an order you wouldn't normally choose. That's always useful because it gives you a different point of view.[1]

Be one who pigeonholes. Look for patterns. They hold the key to unlocking solutions, because they are, or lead to, stories about the people who buy coffee. As you start to see those story patterns, feel free to rearrange the cards.

Second, notice that the mass of information we started with ends up collapsing into five different story lines:
1. image issues regarding good and evil;
2. an image issue regarding maturity
3. a product feature issue - taste;
4. the health issue; and
5. the sales results that grow out of stories 1-4.

Now the question is what do you do with this information?

Be a production planner. By this point you'll notice that all you need to do is add some arrows and you will have a classic "box and arrow" diagram used in pert charts, flow diagrams and electrical design. So add the arrows. Some folks use pre-cut arrows they can slap right on the floor. Of you can use software programs to do it for you. And feel free to re-write, drop, or add items to my own effort. I just want you to note a couple points of interest.

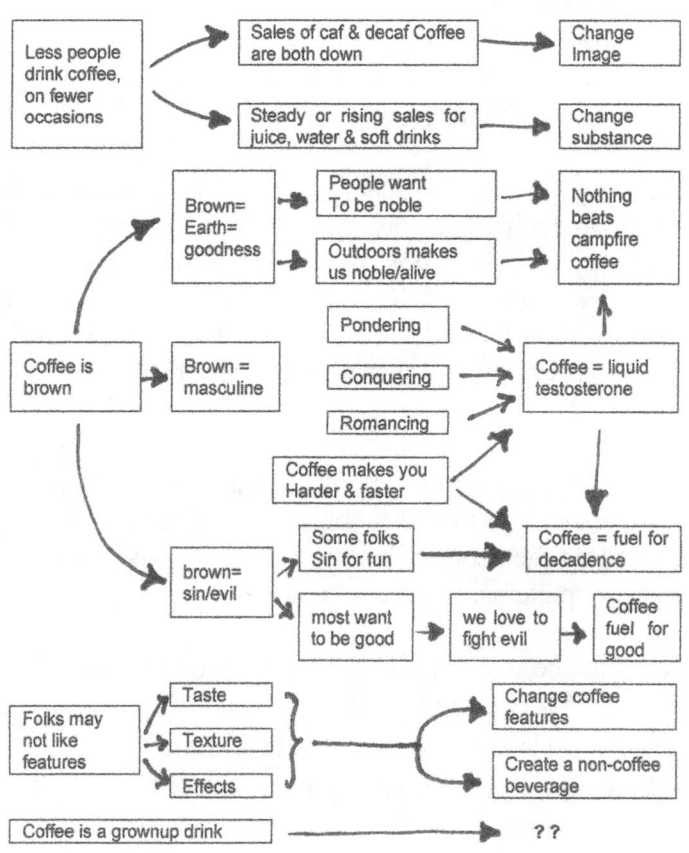

First, the graphic is actually fairly simple. It only has 4 major sections:
1. The problem statement
2. A weird discourse on the color brown
3. A logical discourse on product features
4. A very lonely comment on maturity

Second, notice that the boxes and arrows are trying to lead us to solutions. We're no longer satisfied with simply finding relationships. We want some answers.

Third, notice that I've redefined the coffee issue. I don't have a separate section on health issues. Instead, I took the very things about coffee that are supposed to be bad, and turned them into good things that I can use. That's jumping the wall. There's also a built in back-lash against PC nutrition, sex roles and morality. If you're going over the wall, go over the wall. Don't straddle it.

Step 3 - Focus on the Key Issues

The previous diagram looks like a solution. The weird discourse on the color brown actually led to a definite and attractive solution - reposition coffee as a "guy's drink" - showing the noble warrior romancing his lady love by a fire, with a fairly obvious use of sexual passion. To tell you the truth, I kind of like it. General Food's International Coffees have given a generation of women their own special moments without the use of electrical appliances; but no one is taking care of the men. And men are the biggest consumers of plain old honest-to-god coffee. Sounds great.

But there's a danger to an obvious answer that comes so easily. If it's that obvious, someone else has probably already done it. In fact a number of coffee brands already have; just not with the same level of testosterone I've suggested. So my idea differs only in degree, not in substance. Rats!

Well, it's not a total loss. The idea's good enough to file away until I uncover the real issue. So it's back to the box and arrow diagram for another look. But this time, go over it with a fine-toothed comb, because the solution will usually hinge on a specific box. In our coffee example, we have a sea of boxes, but as I study them once again, one box stands out because it's weird. Notice that the sales of **both** caffeinated and decaffeinated coffee are down. That's pretty interesting. Heck, that's <u>very</u> interesting, because it tells me that health consciousness is <u>not</u> the central issue in coffee sales. If people really cared about health, then decaf coffee sales should be rising while caffeinated sales decline. The fact that **both** varieties of coffee are declining tells us that something other than health issues is kicking us in the shorts.

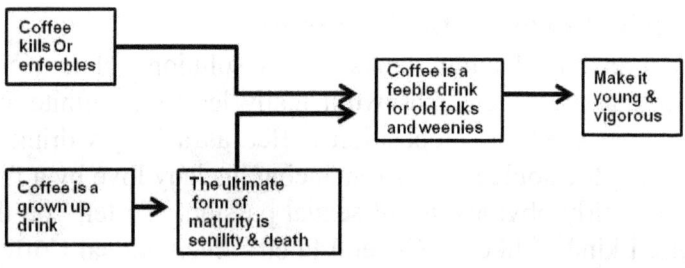

Apparently, consumers are just latching onto the health issue as the best available explanation of their behavior because they can't or won't articulate what's really driving their actions. At this point I realize why I've been keeping the "coffee is a grown-up drink" box, even though it didn't seem to lead anywhere. In short, I have a flash of revelation. My box and arrow diagram needs another section.

That little insight will give us the competitive edge. Every other beverage company is operating on the traditional wisdom trumpeted in the press ... that America is ruled by a new wave of health consciousness. We, however, just redefined the problem.

The pivotal issue is youth, not health. And that realization just pushed us right over the wall that is constraining all our competitors. You, my friend, just hit the jackpot.

Step 4 - Triggering the Ideas

What you need now is specific ideas. But where do you get them? You go back and use those specific techniques we mapped out in the last few chapters. Yeh, I know. I got the cart before the horse. That was done for a reason. Most people are fairly familiar with the idea of managing actions, which is the focus of this chapter. Most people are comfortable with the notion of logically planning and choreographing their activities. But they panic when it comes to generating the ideas that fuel those activities. So I've spent most of the book being a cheerleader and mapmaker for the 4th step in this 6 step process ... because that's where the biggest need lies. So forgive me for not being perfectly linear in putting this book together. Then go back and try some brain storming, mind mapping or pattern searches. You may find something very interesting .... such as the following:
    a. the baby boomers are the primary coffee market;
    b. the baby boomers are aging;
    c. but the baby boomers are the Pepsi generation, and don't want to admit they're getting old;
    d. they remember their parents and other old fogies sitting around guzzling coffee while they waited for the grave;

- e. consequently, coffee isn't a grown up drink, it's a "super-grown-up drink"; an elixir for the aged;
- f. so the baby boomers are drinking less coffee than their parents did at the same age;
- g. and worse yet, the 20-40 year olds won't touch coffee with a 10 foot pole, because they lump it in with bell bottoms and love beads as irrelevant artifacts from a bygone age. Most of them aren't even aware that coffee is an option when drinks are served.

Hmmm, maybe coffee has an image problem, not a health-related problem; and no wonder it doesn't show up in consumer research. How many people make a conscious connection between coffee and growing senile? ..... But now <u>you</u> make the connection, don't you?

What we need now is a little creative market research to cut past consumers' self-ignorance, so that we can confirm this new assumption. But since Folgers isn't financing my work, I won't pursue it any further. Let's just leave it with the observation that it certainly does open a fertile meadow of ideas, doesn't it? Just watch the heavens. The cow pies will start to fall in abundance.

Hmmm –
This could be the Starbucks Story

Step 5 - Order Your Ideas

Congratulations! You're over the wall. You've been inspired. You've gained courage. You've got a tool chest full of techniques, and the willingness to soar. So you've vaulted the wall. And now you stand out in the meadow .... with your foot firmly planted in a cow pie. Sound familiar? This is where I started the previous chapter. By jingo, I've used a flash back technique. I hope you like it. But the question remains. How do you get a handle on all the ideas you've dropped onto the meadow?

WRITE A NOVEL - One way to impose order on your brain is to look at problem solving as a form of storytelling. There's a dilemma, rising action, a resolution, and falling action. So treat it accordingly.

1. Write a title. Sometimes a catchy title will unlock the whole thing for you and put the solution right in your hand. Maybe something like: *"The Coffee-klatch Trap"*
2. Next, write a problem statement in prose. In journalism and fiction it's called "a lead", which lays out the dilemma and gives the reader a reason to read on. Hmmm, maybe we should try something like:
"We're losing our shirts because coffee conjures the image of old ladies discussing the parson's last sermon."
3. Next, sequence the steps that would resolve the dilemma... i.e. what would make the old ladies faint, or run back to church, or give up coffee completely? When you put it that way, it triggers some interesting ideas and images, doesn't it? Okay, but don't just sit there smiling. Write down the steps.
4. Now let's see the conclusion. What causes a troop of vibrant kids to buy & renovate the old house abandoned by the ladies? Who comes in, what do they do, how do they interact ... and most important, how do they like their coffee? And what exactly transpires when that young and noble stud puts his lady love on a bare floor in front of their first fire in the old house? Hmmm? If this sounds vaguely familiar, it's because this kind of voyeurism was laid out in the Imaging Model we covered in an earlier chapter.

REHASH A TECHNIQUE - Some techniques are useful at several stages. So instead of the novelist's approach, you might find that the box and arrow diagram works for you in this stage as well.

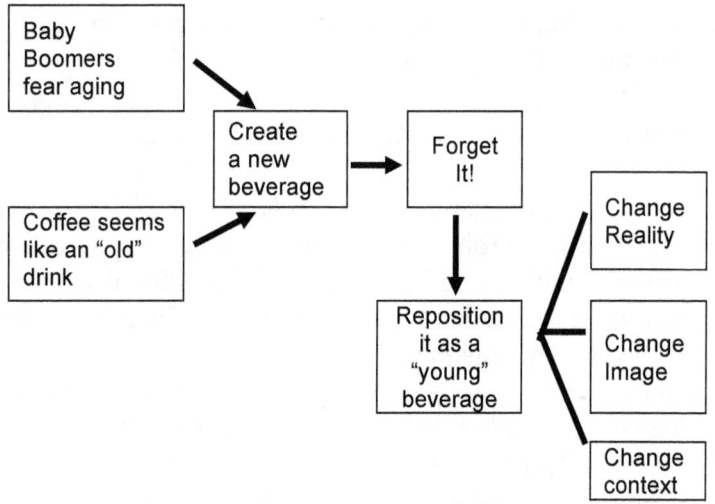

Diagrams are especially effective if you're a visual person, plus they have the added advantage of showing the convergence of factors, and the existence of options. They can even show you where to go when you decide not to pursue one of the options, such as the decision to stick with coffee instead of going into something like herbal tea.

THE FORMAL OUTLINE – A formal outline is solid. It's very linear, and it's also very clear. It shows not only the actions, but also the values that drive them - like the fact that this campaign is clearly male oriented and therefore "sexist" - just about as sexist as International Coffee's projection that women are the only ones interested in flavored coffee and quiet conversation.

> ## FORMAL OUTLNE---THE COFFEE DILEMA
>
> A. Symptom: Coffee sales are declining
> B. The Cause:
>   1. The apparent cause is health consciousness
>   2. The real cause is a fear of aging & irrelevancy
> C. The underlying problems(s)
>   1. Reality – coffee looks, smells, tastes "old"
>   2. Image – coffee means being grown up
>   3. Usage – main use in sedentary settings
> D. Solutions – How to capture the golden ring
>   1. The Product…DON'T CHANGE A THING
>   2. Image
>   - make it a clearly young & "male" drink
>   - make it the stimulant & reward for success
>   - show it as <u>the</u> drink for power & seduction
>   - make it part of everyday labors & life
> E. Bolstering usage occasions
>   1. sponsor rock concerts & stock car racing
>   2. promotional giveaways at sports arenas
>   3. coffee bars at ski lifts and beaches
>   4. joint venture to sell premixed liquor
>   5. promo tie-ins with Home Depot, etc.

When push comes to shove, this kind of clarity and order are pretty good attributes. We know what we're going to do, and why. And so do our in-house critics, which makes debate very focused and, therefore, useful. But formal outlines may not work for you any better now than they did back in 7th grade. So don't force it. Use what feels comfortable to you.

Step 6 - Sell the Solution
If you're one of those rare hermit geniuses, you're just about done. All you have to do is "do". However, the rest of us live in families and/or other organizations, and can't "do" on our own. We have to sell other people on the worth of our solution. That means we've got to communicate in a persuasive manner. Here are some tips.

THE READER'S LIST - Remember something very crucial. No one else has been out in the meadow with you. They're all safely behind the wall. They've missed out on everything you've been through. So not a single one of your "of courses" hold water for them. That means you've got to lead them by the hand. You have to go back inside their wall and start from where they are, not from where you are, or even from where you'd like them to be. One way to help yourself do this is to role play. Write down the questions you'd have if you were the other guy. Then arrange the questions in the order they're likely to occur. As an example, let me share the reader's list I generated for this book.
  1. What is creativity?
  2. How is it unique?
  3. Can I do it?
  4. Is it worth the effort?
  5. How exactly do I get it & use it?
  6. What will it do to me ... and SO WHAT?

Your questions might not have been exactly the same, and they may not have occurred in the same order. But the exercise made me think about you, not me, and the result has been a fairly persuasive effort. How do we know? You're still reading.

THE CONTENT STORY BOARD - If you try to sell your idea by going through a blow by blow replication of how you got it, you won't sell many ideas. As Craig Stewart - the noted training consultant - said, "Folks don't want to hear the labor pains, they just want to see the baby". So cut out most of the details and focus on the highlights.

One way to do this is to use a content story board. In essence, your report, presentation, or informal pitch is going to have a beginning (the problem statement), a middle (the pivotal discovery that solves the problem) and an end (suggested solutions and a projection). List all your information on the left of a page, and transfer the pertinent bits into the three columns on the right so that they'll make a gripping and convincing narrative. You can even number the points in order of their appearance.

	Begin	Mid	End
The Industry			
- coffee sales down (caf & de-caf)	2		
- Fruit juice sales are up	2		
- Bottled water sales are up	2		
- Soft drink sales are steady	2		
The Market			
-Fewer people are drinking it	3		
- Fewer coffee occasions	4		
Caffeine = stimulant			
- Health issues may be cause	5	1	
- Health issues are a sham	- - -	3	
Color brown = mother earth			
- Nobility is in vogue	- - -	- - -	1A
- Being outdoors = nobility	- - -	- - -	1B
- Campfire coffee is best	- - -	- - -	1C
- Good/evil struggle	- - -	- - -	- - -
- Good folks drink coffee	- - -	- - -	3C
Color brown = sin/evil			
- People sin to have fun	- - -	- - -	3B
- But they don't want to pay the price	- - -	- - -	3A
Color brown = masculinity	- - -	- - -	2A
- Action & seduction	- - -	- - -	2B
Coffee is grown-up drink	- - -	4	
- Kills & enfeebles	- - -	5	
- Makes you senile	- - -	6	

But notice something interesting. A good deal of what you know, and have done, ends up on the cutting room floor.
- Part of that is due to the "labor pains/baby" syndrome.
- But part of it is due to the fact that some of what you've done and thought is just too weird for your audience. Remember, they're back behind their own wall. They haven't been out in the meadow with you. So if you're trying to convince the Romans to do something, you darn well better speak Latin, not Martian.

When all is said and done, you've come up with the "Taste for Action" campaign ... aimed squarely at the 29 year-old male who wants to be as noble as a saint, as powerful as an emperor, and as randy as a politician. Coffee is the chemical jumpstart and reward for a young and vigorous life of full masculinity.

PIZZAZZ - Now you're finally ready to attach the bells and whistles. Make a prototype. Create the four-color computer graphics. Hire the band and order the cocktails. Just remember that 9 times out of 10, the content is going to carry the day. Pizzazz simply gets their attention. But in a world of communication overload, just getting their attention is very important. A couple of tips:

- **Hit the other person's hot buttons.** If employee turnover is their chief concern, put "repositioning coffee and its effect on employee turnover" in the title, or at a minimum underline it in the first paragraph. If they like data, give them tons of numbers ... but put them in an appendix. Don't clutter the narrative. Just drop in a conspicuous number here and there to get them salivating.

- **Tell a story**. Nobody cares about coffee, itself. But everyone will care about the person who makes, sells or uses that coffee when you treat your idea within the context of a story. Create characters. Mention people's names. Show how the idea affects them. Invoke the welfare, fame and wealth that various parties stand to gain. Give the other person someone to care about and they'll care about your idea as well.

♦ **Write with a little flair.** When words drone on and on they start to look like wall paper with a very small pattern. It'll put your audience to sleep, or drive them to stop reading or listening.

And there's one piece of pizzazz that should be self-evident ... your idea. Show it proudly and completely, then stand back and let it shine a little.

That's Structure

There you have it. Uncle Joe's 6 Easy steps to success.

1. *C*ollect information
2. *O*rder the information
3. *F*ocus on the key issues
4. *T*rigger ideas
5. *O*rder the ideas
6. *S*ell the Solution

It's absurd to think I captured the totality of creativity in such a compressed instrument. But what do you think? Did I come close? If so, use it. If not, make up your own. By this point you're as creative as I am.[2]

End Notes

1. A number of the structural techniques in this chapter have been extolled by writing professors, editors and functional philosophers for years. I'd say they're part of common knowledge and the public domain. However, someone other than me ought to get some credit, because I didn't originate the whole batch myself. So I'll cite Donald Murray, <u>Write to Learn</u>, 1984, CBS College Publishing, New York. He's one of the many authors who have written about structuring thought.

2. I don't know squat about coffee. I don't even drink the stuff. Neither have I researched the coffee market. In short, everything I've said about coffee is purely armchair psychology and speculation. My only purpose was to illustrate a few points. So, for goodness sake, don't sell the farm to get into the coffee market based on what you've read here. Then again ... it kind of made sense, didn't it? So if this copyrighted idea actually works for you - just send me a thank you note ... and 5 % of the increase in gross revenue.

14
WHAT ABOUT MY HEAD?
(CREATIVITY AND PERSONALITY)

Up to this point, we've been talking about creativity as though it were a specimen in the laboratory. We've dissected it. We've talked about its components. We've dispassionately looked at the process and structure involved. And in so doing, we've held it at arm's length so it wouldn't sweat all over us. Well that's about to change, because this chapter is going to talk about creativity at a very personal and intimate level. We're going to talk about what it does to your head.

Making a commitment to creativity is exhilarating. But it's a major step. Like other major steps - such as getting married, having a baby or buying a house - getting creative will change your life. So before you jump in hook, line, and sinker, it's wise to get an idea of what lies ahead.

You can limit the surprises. Creativity itself is fairly complex, so you don't want the added complexity of being distracted by unexpected changes in your personality and behavior. If you know what's coming, it doesn't throw you when it appears. Discuss it ahead of time with others.

You can help other people adjust to you, if you're aware of what's going on in your own head. That's crucial, because you don't leave society behind when you vault the wall. You still have an obligation to be a useful member of relationships, and by making yourself understandable to others, you help those relationships remain productive.

You can guard against being manipulated. Is that important? Go ask Walt Disney's ghost. Walt developed such a high need for affirmation that he trusted an unscrupulous film distributor who pretended to worship his talent. Then the distributor walked away with the copyright on Walt's only money maker - a cartoon duck named Waldo. As a result, Disney went into bankruptcy, where he would have stayed except for his brainstorm about a talking rodent. He was lucky. Most people aren't.

Those are the three major reasons why this chapter is important. I also have a fourth: **self-knowledge is the door to greatness.** Taking a look at your own mind is like walking into a glorious cathedral. The sunlight filters through the gothic arches and stained glass windows, showing you the intricate complexity that makes you fascinating and capable. And that sense of self fuels the enormous effort that greatness demands.

Walking into that cathedral also allows you to see how all the pieces fit together into an integrated whole. No experience you've ever had is wasted. No personal struggle or triumph sits isolated in some nostalgic past. It's all part of the masonry of the mind and when you tap into it, that personal history sharpens your talents in the present and the future.

The question, of course, is how do we break into our own cathedral? Without on-site guidance from a counselor that's tough to do. So let's do something far easier. We'll sneak into someone else's cathedral, instead, and maybe we can learn a few things there that will help us with our own lives.

To do this, I've chosen to look at the ultra-creative folks; the people who far exceed the level of creativity that most of us can achieve. I do this for two reasons. First, they make the issues more clear because their personalities are more extreme. We'll get a pristine view that makes a point, then we'll see what the applications are for our own lives. The second reason for looking at the ultra-creatives is that they're fascinating and entertaining.

Geniuses and Magicians

A creative genius is someone you and I could be just as good as, if only we were twice as good as we are. We can understand what he did, and how he did it. The marvel resides in the simple fact that he was the first person to figure something out.

A creative magician, however, is another matter entirely. Even if we comprehend what exactly he's done, the process by which he did it is still beyond us. We couldn't be as good as that guy even if we were 100 times better than we are.

Richard Feynman was just such a creature. To begin with, he was the father of The Theory of Quantum Electro-Dynamics, which is one of those "grand theories" in physics that explains just about everything: the behavior of subatomic particles, light, electricity, atomic movement, magnetism and why your washer always eats one sock.

But the theory itself isn't the most interesting aspect of Feynman. That's merely the "what". The real mind blower is the "how".[1] You see, Feynman violated the first rule of science - he developed his grand theory without using equations.

Instead, he invented something called Feynman Diagrams, which were a combination of cartoons, hieroglyphics, and chicken scratches that traced and predicted the movement of particles. And this gibberish has now been adopted by other scientists as a major tool in the quantum physics world.

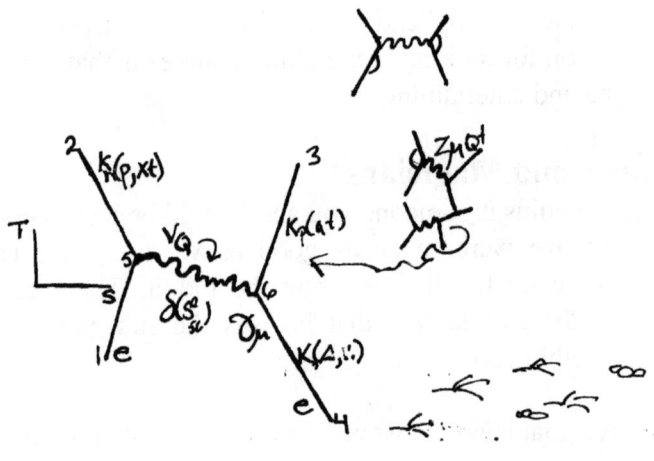

Why? Because a central tenet of quantum physics is that a particle can move from one point to another (perhaps light years away) without actually traveling across the space in between. Even the most advanced mathematics can't cope with that violation of standard logic. So imagine that. The symbolic scrawl of a 3 year-old may actually hold the secrets of the universe.

Newton, Descartes, Einstein, and Feynman all left their mark by inventing new mathematical or logical tools. That's their real glory, not the specific problems they solved. Why is that? Because the rest of us get our ideas from the tools we see lying around.

My son was a perfectly normal human being until the first time he saw a coil of rope. Without any instruction, and without the ability to even read the Boy Scout Handbook, he tied up my entire house. Booby traps for burglars were everywhere. The furniture was all securely tied in place. And the second story of his playhouse fort had such a dense web of rope that it went beyond hammock status to the point of being a third floor. My son was creative, but he was inspired by the creative magician who invented the first tool - the rope itself. And sitting out there in the universe right now is a kid who'll actually perfect space leaps, once she gets inspired by a Feynman diagram.

The Magician's Mind
Magicians spend their entire lives outside the wall. As a result, they can get a little strange. If his biographers are accurate, Feynman is a good example. According to them, he was a very interesting fellow.

1. He was irreverent to the point of rudeness. He played the bongos and occasionally used them to drown out critics, peers and students during heated discussions.

2. He showed absolute disdain and condescension toward politicians, bureaucrats and most peers. In short, he hated authority figures, heroes and hero worship. Yet he wrote two autobiographies in which he was clearly the hero, or god.

3. And if he be a god, it must be Bacchus. His diet, exercise and sleep patterns were outside the norms established by the surgeon general.

4. He refused to do secondary research. He never cared what anyone else had thought, discovered or proved about any topic. He simply started from ground zero on every issue and reinvented science on his way to solving a specific problem.

5. He hated all the proofs, corollaries and step by step mathematical logic that was drummed into our heads back in 10th grade geometry, and which professional mathematicians actually use. He saw proofs as stupid techniques which tied dim-witted scientists to the problem, instead of focusing their attention on discovering a solution. Consequently, his solutions came from grand intuitive leaps rather than from the plodding logic used by his peers.

6. He never met a thigh he didn't like. He was a voracious consumer of superficial (and should we say, "creative") sexual encounters. Even in his 60's he was still cruising bars picking up girls. Yet he had been a devoted husband, to the point of lovingly nursing his wife through a lengthy terminal illness.

7. Finally, he refused to be trapped or tagged as a specialist, in a scientific world that demands specialization. In fact his biggest moment in the sun occurred outside his field of expertise. Remember the explosion of the space shuttle "Challenger"? And remember the televised hearings to determine the cause of that disaster? Every scientist in America showed up with awe-inspiring floor to ceiling stacks of computer print outs, analyses and theoretical projections that indicated, suggested and guessed what maybe coulda, kinda shoulda, sorta.... Then after they'd all failed to explain the explosion, Feynman showed up with a glass of ice water. He stuck a rubber O-ring in it, and with his best "you dumb schmucks" smile, he broke the O-ring like a dry pretzel, thus proving that cold weather had caused the problem.

Believe it or not, this little jaunt through the head of Richard Feynman leads us into some observations which can be exploited to aid our own creativity.

Manic Highs & Lows

Feynman was a little odd. But he was not alone. Psychologist Kay Jamison performed an in-depth study of bona fide creative geniuses in art and literature; those who were either members of the Royal Academy of Arts or who had received the Pulitzer, Nobel or some other prestigious award. Her findings were stunning: 89% of them exhibited the classic signs of manic-depression, and 38% of them had been institutionalized or chemically treated for the disorder. That's seven times the rate in the rest of society.

We can grieve for the crushing lows these folks experience, but we also envy the incredible productive highs that complete the cycle. George Frideric Handel wrote "The Messiah" in a mere 24 days. And Sir Walter Scott knocked out <u>Ivanhoe</u> in a little more than two weeks. Hemingway did his best work during manic highs, as did Balzac, Virginia Woolf, and F. Scott Fitzgerald. And Beethoven did most of his work in the dementia of a caged manic beast.

What should you do? How does all this apply to you and me? All we want to do is find a nifty way to increase market share by 15%, or cut the grass without sweating. Well, here's the point. Don't get scared by the emotional ups and downs that come with creativity. And if you do happen to suffer from a touch of manic-depression, bravo. You've got the seeds of greatness in you. Put the tranquilizers away and let your mind achieve that pristine focus that God only gives his special children.[2] You realize of course, that you need to take that last piece of advice with a grain of salt, right?

Refrigerator Art, and Mirrors

Most of us try to be wonderful at what we do. But what good is all the effort unless there's some way for us to know when we've succeeded? So the question becomes, where do we look to find out ... the mirror or the refrigerator?

> **Some of us look in the mirror**, see the reflection of who we are and what we've done - and make peace with ourselves regardless of what anyone else thinks. We're driven by self image.
>
> **Some of us look at the refrigerator door**. If Mom has proudly posted our work there we know we're a hit. If not, it doesn't matter what we see in the mirror, we're crushed. We are driven, and in some measure

controlled, by others' reactions to us. Nothing is ever good enough, until someone else says so.

Most people seem to be satisfied by their own self image. We know this because the suicide rate is so low. After all, most organizations don't give enough praise and reward to keep a sparrow alive; especially if the sparrow needs the affirmation of seeing their work on a refrigerator door.

Creativity, however, tends to unleash the child in us that needs that kind of affirmation. If you've been toiling out in the meadow all day, you've also been toiling out there in the absence of any benchmarks whatsoever. Remember, you're outside the wall, outside of any known form of civilization. So the kid in you wants to come home each night, crawl back over the wall and be assured that everything is alright because you "done good".

What should you do? Enjoy it. Run, show your work to someone. Post it on the wall. Hell, tape it on the refrigerator. That's what Susie did with the contract for my first book the day it arrived, and she put a huge gold star on it to boot. It was the strangest thing. That hadn't happened to me since I was a kid. It actually felt real good.

When the Refrigerator Becomes a Throne

Feynman was a piece of work, as evidenced by the logical absurdity of his books. In effect, he proclaimed "There are no heroes in this world ... and I am chief among them." His anti-hero bias makes sense if you realize that heroes are simply the kings that reside within the old wall. Consequently regicide (killing the king) is at least figuratively part of vaulting the wall. But if heroes are a major impediment to progress, why would Feynman turn around and portray himself as exactly that in his own books?

Ah ... now we cut to the nub of humanity, because Feynman was not alone. Many other geniuses have done the same thing. Henry Ford was like that. So were Martin Luther and Teddy Roosevelt; and Sigmund Freud was probably the worst. He railed against the established heroes on his way over the wall. But as soon as he'd built his own wall out there in the meadow he declared himself unquestioned monarch of all he surveyed. In fact, he was so rigid that he chased away his best disciples, such as Carl Jung, for minor disagreements with his dogma.

The problem was that these guys had wandered so far away from the old wall that they couldn't get back to check out the refrigerator door. So they built their own refrigerator, posted their work, and declared their refrigerator off-limits to anyone else. They'd crowned themselves king.

What should you do? Control your need to be king. When you don't let other folks have a shot at the refrigerator door, you're stopping creativity dead in its tracks. So lighten up. There's plenty of room on that door.

Sex

Ever since Chapter 1, I've been telling you that creativity only comes when you relax enough to release it. And there's no question that sex releases a lot of tension. So maybe old Richard Feynman was on to something. In fact --- research data, anecdotes and personal observation all show us that sexuality and creativity are closely related.

A person's natural sexual tendencies are exaggerated when they're being creative. The disinterested person moves toward complete celibacy. The interested person becomes a bedroom carnivore. And those who are normally kinky become, how do we say? ... downright pretzel-like.

> Carl Jung put his finger on why life works this way.[3] Fantasy is a key ingredient in the hunt, seduction and ritual of sex. Fantasy is also a primary source of creative ideas. So fantasy is the bridge that carries our brain back and forth between functional creativity and the rest of our life. As Jung said, "... without this playing with fantasy no creative work has ever come to birth."

Sexual fantasy simply jump starts the creative engine. The problem is it's a little tough on spouses. They lose interest, not to mention patience after the sixth such encounter each day. And that's why so many creative people have affairs: that, plus the fact that nothing matches the fantasy of seducing a new quarry.

What should you do? If you're stumped, take a sex break. Look down a blouse or up a skirt. Or if you're on the other side of the preference fence, check out a nice set of buns in a pair of jeans, or count the hairs on someone's chest. And don't forget to flirt like a banshee. The problem with the PC paranoia about sexual harassment is that firms are becoming so sterile and constricted that creativity is being robbed of even the most harmless and safe aspect of human sexuality, simple flirtation.

Lighten up, America. You have nothing to lose but your inhibitions. Or your panties. Helen Gurley Brown, the head, heart and driving engine behind Cosmopolitan magazine, was fond of the weekly ritual of "pantsing the girls" around her office. Even as an octogenarian, she recommended such activities as a way to boost morale, creativity and productivity. Admittedly, Ms. Brown's recommendation is a bit extreme. But it is not absurd. You can feel an incredible level of sexual energy when you roam the halls of a creative firm. Aren't you glad the PC police have declared little old ladies off limits? Sometimes they impart a little wisdom. If Bill Gates had made that recommendation he'd have been crucified.

Diet

Experts prescribe an amazing array of nature's bounty as creative stimulants. The potassium in bananas is supposed to work wonders. Apples are also highly recommended. But I think their major benefit is the pectin which clogs the system and limits disruptions for bathroom breaks. Then of course there are the nuts, cheeses, cereals and other squirrel foods that are all high in fiber. And on and on the list goes. My own personal belief is that these experts all have their heads stuck up a lunch bag. They wouldn't recognize a creative buzz if it bit them on the nose.

What you need is sugar. Nothing beats a sugar high for instant energy and clarity of thought. It clears the cobwebs, straightens the spine and energizes the wits. And for goodness sake people ... it tastes terrific. Its biggest disadvantage is that the benefits of a sugar high are short lived, and the inevitable crash can fog the mind and fatigue the body. That's why the experts say you should stay away from it.

Think about that for a minute. The same logic would lead us to avoid using cars, because all they'd do is take us 100 miles away from home and then run out of gas. The experts seem to forget that God invented gas stations to take care of that problem. Well, He also invented refrigerators to take care of the sugar problem. So stop in regularly and fill 'er up.

What should you do? My own recommendation is that you put some Cokes on ice, lay out a plate of Oreo's and keep the fires burning. Then at 2:00 a.m. you can cut yourself off and crash into a blissful sleep by 2:30 a.m. My presentation here is a bit flippant. But the research bears it out. Creative people have atrocious eating habits, from a nutritional stand point. They guzzle coffee, mainline sugar and cram down the junk food. Yes, these things will eventually kill laboratory rats. But is your goal to keep the rat in you alive, or to accomplish something with your life? The bottom line ... eat what makes you happy.

Gimmicks

Lord Byron often composed his poetry on the naked backs of his lovers, while he (how do we say this tactfully) penetrated to the heart of the matter. Martin Luther wrote his great works wrapped in a fur coat, with a warm tankard of beer, beside a raging fire ... in the blistering heat of summer. Descartes did his best thinking while sitting outside in his underwear, in the dead of winter. Winston Churchill held meetings with his cabinet ministers while he soaked in the bathtub; a glistening Buddha with a cigar. And Ben Franklin was famous for startling state visitors with his nightly "air-baths", which he enjoyed au natural.

The list goes on and on, but the point is that every creative person seems to have a quirk. Many of them are sexual or at least sensual in nature, which reinforces what I said earlier about sex and creativity. However, not all the quirks are - or need be - sexual. Some folks chop wood for their gimmick. Thomas Edison used fly fishing. Pope John Paul II relied on long walks in the woods. Legs are my thing. I curl one leg beneath me as I sit composing this book. If not, I can't think, much less write. I'll switch from one leg to the other. But I notice that I'm usually sitting on my right leg while I compose ideas, and on my left leg while I work out charts, diagrams or tables. I don't want to give too much credit to other researchers and writers, but this observation seems to fit in with the theory of right brain and left brain activity.

What should you do? Get yourself a gimmick. Take your shoes off and wiggle your toes while you work. Open a window in winter. Wear your underwear inside out, or on your head. Just dink around with this technique for a while and you'll find something that clicks. It's like a physiological signal to your brain that it's time to kick into gear. It's also a marvelous way to torment your spouses, by convincing them that the activity is necessary for the good of creativity and therefore mankind as a whole.

Self-Indulgent Pleasure
Take a minute here and ponder what I've suggested. Go nuts. Have sex. Main line sugar. And get a gimmick. What do they all have in common? They are intense personal pleasures. They are indulgences that most people deny themselves because they live rigidly within the walls of what's acceptable and proper. One of the major preparations and fuels for creativity is your own mood.

What should you do? Find something that brings you pleasure. A hot bubble bath may work for some. A foot massage may work for others. A friend of mine who's a successful editorial cartoonist swears by acupuncture, of all things. And Walt Disney used to get a nightly rub down by his European masseuse. Johan Sebastian Bach found his pleasure in devout prayer, <u>and</u> the fact that he sired about 24 children. But that harkens back to a technique we don't need to belabor.

Be a Busy-Body

Feynman couldn't keep his nose out of other people's business. Neither could most of the great inventors throughout history. Alexander Graham Bell was a speech pathologist, not a mechanic. Eli Whitney (father of the cotton gin) was a school teacher, not a farmer. Gauguin, the famous painter of naked Tahitians, was a banker. Each of them dabbled outside their professional fields for the same reason any busy-body wanders into someone else's yard. They did it for their own pleasure. Bell and Whitney were both trying to impress chicks: Bell, his fiancée; and Whitney the planter's wife where he boarded. Gauguin just wanted some cheap thrills.

What should you do? Branch out. Your biggest contribution will probably come out̲side your area of professional expertise. That's because you've been so thoroughly trained that you can't see the forest for the trees in your own backyard. So if you're in the finance department, your best ideas might relate to marketing. And if you're a schoolteacher, you could probably write a pretty good movie script.

Once you start nosing around like that, you become the ultimate busybody. We call them "generalists", and society would be lost without them. The ancient philosophers called this approach "Nephishism", which is a great word for making an impression on the cocktail circuit. It represents a marvelous life style; the kind of holistic, jack-of-all-trades approach to life that leads to fulfillment and self-actualization. Thomas Jefferson was a classic example of this kind of life. He dabbled in everything and personified what we now call "The Renaissance Man".

Most of us have a "path not taken" - that other vocation we always fantasized about, and still do at times. Don't let it rot. Either chase it, or find a way to incorporate it into your "normal" activities. That's probably where your true genius lies.

Kiss Off the Experts

The average U.S. organization spends 5% of its time making decisions and 40% of its time implementing them. The remaining 55% of its time is spent rationalizing its decisions by thoroughly checking precedents, studying prior and current research, and subjecting ideas to test markets.[4] We live in a timid world. Isn't it refreshing to encounter a guy like Feynman who says, "Screw the experts, no one knows better than me."

What should you do? If you're not the owner of your organization, you probably can't get away with Feynman's behavior. However, unless you adopt a little bit of that attitude, your creative work won't be much good. As Einstein pointed out, great ideas come from revelation and insight, not from plodding through other people's work. But Einstein also said that once you get an idea, make it look like the result of laborious logic and footwork so other people will think it has credibility.

The Creative's Ego

It sounds as though creativity will turn you into an ego-maniac, doesn't it? You long for refrigerator fame. You crown yourself emperor of the universe. You kiss off the experts, and go your merry way. Well, before jumping to conclusions, you have to see those factors in the total context of being creative; at which point we discover that the egos of most creative people are really fairly tame. The real breakthroughs in life often bewilder the originator himself.

They seem to come out of nowhere, and they occur so instantaneously that the originator is often flabbergasted at the massiveness of his own accomplishment. Consequently, most of them downplay their own contribution.

- ◆ Carl Jung attributed his psychological breakthroughs to the fantasy of play, not to his own brilliance.
- ◆ Einstein credited God-given imagination, passing the credit to genetics rather than to his own efforts.
- ◆ Newton, at a loss for a more comprehensible explanation, credited an elemental force of nature – a falling apple.
- ◆ Edison refused to accept his own genius and claimed that his success came from 99% perspiration and only 1% inspiration, as though anyone could have done it, if they'd just tried hard enough.
- ◆ And Paul MacCready ducked all credit for his inventions by proclaiming that the real glory goes to the engineers who work out the details.

What should you do? Don't be afraid of your own ego. Make peace with the fact that your ego will bounce all over the place. Sometimes you will stand in awe of yourself and expect others to do the same. At other times, you will see yourself as the lowly earthen vessel for someone else's brilliance; all the while hoping that your friends will refute that image and push you back onto your pedestal.

THE NOSREDNA SUCCESS FORMULA

You've been quite active in this chapter. You acquired an organic mental illness. You had sex while enjoying a sugar high. You co-opted your significant other into amusing perversities for the sake of mankind. And it was all done in the name of creativity. That's like getting a license to steal.

But I haven't said a thing about how you think, have I? Instead, I focused on how you feel. Why? It goes back to Nephishism, that holistic approach to life. The fact is that you can't separate your thoughts and feelings into nice neat packages; they're part and parcel of one another. So, I just wanted to map out what life might be like if you go after creativity lock, stock and barrel. Whether you achieve genius status or not, you'll brush up against a little bit of everything we've looked at. So, now you have foreknowledge. But that knowledge carries a burden. Now that you know, there are a few things you should do.

Step 1 – Relax

The first thing to do is relax. Any of the oddities you develop will actually be pretty minor. A case in point ... I recently talked to a veteran commercial artist who told me that he hadn't really shifted into high gear as a creative person until two years ago. As we talked, it came out that this creative surge at work happened to coincide with the onset of his consuming interest in making guitars by hand. I smiled. His success occurred on the day that he had become nephishistic, by choice, not by ritual.

Step 2 – Family

The second thing to do is tend the home fires, so that your spouse and family don't suddenly wake up to a stranger. This part's fairly easy, and sometimes fun. You can start by having those significant others read this chapter. Better still, have them read the whole book. Or if you really want to do it up right, read it out loud to one another. There will be occasional chuckles as family members recognize attributes. But most important, there will be some good old fashioned discussion.

An added bonus is validity. For some reason, seeing personality traits officially noted in a published book makes them credible. They're no longer personal oddities, possessed by you alone. Now they're a bona fide attribute of someone who's worthwhile - an honest to goodness creative person.

My wife and I are a case in point. Susie lives in the concrete world. I live on the other side of the wall. One day I stumbled across a book called Please Understand Me, by David Keirsey and Marilyn Bates, and it changed our relationship. The book was an armchair psychology book, focusing on the various personality types, and it thankfully included a section on creative personalities. As we read through one personality type that represented a mere 1% of the population, Susie began to laugh. Then in wonderment she asked, "So you don't act this way just to be a jerk?"

Since I sit within only 1% of the population, Susie had never met anyone else like me. So she had always assumed that my personal quirks were purposely developed just to irritate her. That all changed when she saw that I rated coverage in a book, because there were other people like me. Even if it was only 1% of the population, that was good enough for her. Now she thinks I'm intriguing. Better still - she has become my chief sounding board, my best critic, and in all respects my complete partner. That's not bad for reading one little book out loud.

Step 3 – Educate

The third thing to do is educate your peers. Write a synopsis of this particular book, and circulate it around the office for everyone's edification ... and don't forget to include Dr. Anderson's interesting observations on personality.

That way I serve as your front man. You could also conduct a seminar on being creative. It's a hot topic right now and you'll get brownie points for being on the cutting edge. You'll also get a chance to educate your peers on who and what you are, without going through the discomfort of a public confessional.

Step 4 - Self Control

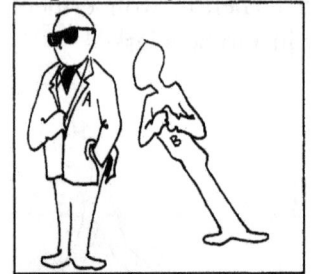

Finally - control yourself. There are wolves in the woods. They'll stroke you. They'll cajole you. And if you let them, they'll eat you for breakfast. The grownup in you has to be in charge when you're dealing with other folks. Otherwise the child part will give away the farm just to see their work on the refrigerator. Always remember, if something seems too good to be true, it is exactly that. So look at praise with a discerning eye. Not bitter. Not distrustful. Just don't let it fog your vision. Other people will want something from you, so a little sucking up on their part is perfectly normal and proper.

But when it moves from healthy sucking up to slavish worship - beware. The trap is about to spring. Snake oil salesmen are smooooth for a reason. They deal in grease.

On the other side of the fence, don't let the critics get to you either. Some people are extremely sensitive to your need for exposure on the figurative refrigerator. So they'll play the role of judgmental Mom to the hilt. Nothing's ever good enough for praise, unless you sell your soul to them. Don't put up with that kind of coercion. Find another refrigerator ... or pay more attention to your mirror.

****

See? That wasn't too painful. In fact, it was kind of interesting. You got a little ancient philosophy. You got a little current psychology. You got some great words to toss around at cocktail parties. And you got a little insight into your own life as a normal, creative working stiff. I hope it helps. Now, I feel a conclusion coming on. So fasten your seatbelts and let's see if I can make a smooth landing.

End Notes

1. *The information on Richard Feynman can be found in: James Gleick, <u>Genius: The Life and Science of Richard Feynman</u>, Pantheon, 1992. For a brief review, see "The Physicist as Magician", <u>Time</u>, December 7, 1992, pp. 76, 81*

2. *A nice little summary of Kay Jamison's research can be found in "The Ups and Downs of Creativity", <u>Time</u>, October 8, 1984, p.76 . Or you might just like to go to the horse's mouth and read the original: Kay Jamison and F.K. Goodwin, <u>Manic-Depressive Illness</u>, 1985*

3. *Carl Gustav Jung, <u>Psychological Types</u>, 1923*

4. *These figures are my own expert opinion, based on observations from a consultant's perspective. It's tough to get good empirical data on issues such as this.*

15
WALL VAULTING
(IT'S TIME TO LEAVE THE NEST)

Creativity causes change.
And change terrifies people.

Change is the act of letting go of one thing so you can take hold of another --- which is fine, unless you're comfortable with the thing you've already got in your hand. And most people are, no matter how much they complain about it. The devil you know is better than the devil you don't know. Uncertainty is the thing we hate most in life.

Change is like divorce. Someone is always worse off after it occurs. Of course, one of the spouses is also better off --- a lot better off. Here's the rub. We know that the one initiating the change will usually be the one who's better off, which means the other guy is left holding the bag, so to speak.

Finally, change is always negative at first, for everyone. Nothing is ever where it used to be, where it's "supposed" to be. It's true of budget allocations, resources, tools, silverware --- you name it. Life just isn't the same and we're all off kilter for a while until our systems get used to the new world order.

In short, our old way of life dies every time someone in the vicinity is creative. This is especially true when we aren't the change agent ourselves. So it turns out that grief is the most useful model for coping with creativity. Grief progresses in five clearly discernible steps. People's reaction to change (and therefore their reaction to creativity) follows the same path.

The Grief Cycle
The first response is usually "Did I hear that right? That can't be right. No. That's absurd. Who could think such a thing? That's just stupid!" This is usually the symptom most associated with paradigm shift – we simply deny the thing that stands right in front of us.

When it sinks in, the next stage unleashes various stages of rage; from cold calculated resistance plans and pledges to yelling and picketing. A gun is usually a great comfort to someone in this stage. Bombs also bring peace of mind.

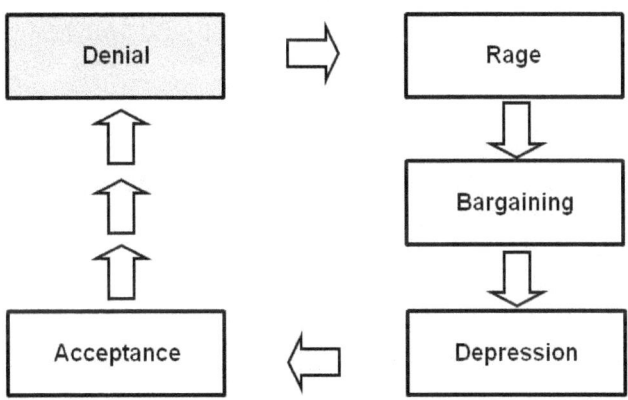

One wonders if the Muslim world is simply suffering from all the technological and economic changes that have occurred in the past 20 years. Perhaps the best way to fight terrorism is to teach the Arabs what the Indians and Filipinos know and let them have the concession for outsourced computer work.

When you fail to shout down or kill the source of change, you eventually try to reason with it – you know – bribe it. We'll even make a deal with cancer "If you let my Mom live, I'll become a Sunday School teacher". In fact, if Al Qaeda survives long enough, the world will eventually negotiate with it. It is inevitable. Look at how we made accommodations with Iran and North Korea, despite enormous saber rattling between 1980 and 2007.

Regardless of how successful our bargaining goes, we can never get change to disappear. Once the genie is out of the bottle, it simply refuses to go back in. As a result, depression always sets in as we deal with the fact that nothing will ever be exactly the same. We'll moan a little and cry a little, and tell nostalgic stories about the way things used to be – back in the day when life made sense and people had moral fiber. And then we'll grow quiet and stare off into the distance.

Then after a while, the new nonsense starts to become familiar. Then it becomes the norm. And eventually we accept it and start to lead a vibrant life inside the new reality. If we're lucky we'll get a few good years of that before some other jerk comes along and vomits some new "creativity" all over our new shoes. And then we're right back in the stew, moving from disbelief to rage and on through the cycle again. And again. And again.

If you're the change agent – realize that this is going to happen, to some degree, every single time you broach a new idea. And the reaction will be stronger, and the cycle time longer, the more creative you have been. That's why organizations, cultures and religions usually change <u>very</u> slowly. On the other hand, technology can change with breathtaking speed because atoms don't have a grief cycle. Of course, the scientists who study them do, as Einstein found out.

So even if you're a physicist or chemist, you'd be well served to anticipate the grief cycle and plot a strategy for plodding your way through the resistance you will encounter. And realize that while the attacks and criticism will be very personal, it's not really personal. They simply hate you, and fear you, as an agent of Satan.

If you're NOT the change agent – realize that your reactions may have little to do with the merits of the idea. You may simply be racing through the grief cycle. As a result, you may want to temper your response and not slaughter the messenger. In fact, I would go so far as to suggest the 9 Commandments of Coping with Change.

1. Agree that everyone here loves the _____ (church, company, country, faith, party, whatever. YOU fill in the blank.) to the same degree. Even more important, a benevolent providence loves us all the same. When we forget that, we start sounding like politicians at election time.

2. Never call names, or cast aspersions, or turn the discussion into personal spats. That kind of behavior is an obstacle to resolving the problem and makes you look like a thumb-sucking 8th grade brat. How's that for name calling?

3. Never assume that you know the other guy's motivation. Only he can tell you what that is. The best you can do is taking his word for it.

4. Wait for your turn to talk. Then be brief.

5. Listen to what the other guy actually says. Most of us don't listen. We're just marking time, waiting for the other guy to take a breath so we can counterattack.

6. Focus on the functional, not the moral point of view. No one compromises on morals. Once it becomes a moral issue the only possible resolution is the other guy's death (or yours).

7. Look for common ground. Shared values, vision, goals give us a place to start.

8. If tempers flare, separate and take a break—with the promise to return to the table, at a specific time.

9. Discipline yourself to say "My, isn't that fascinating. Why do you think that?"

Let's imagine for a moment that you've paid attention to the material in this chapter. Let's also imagine that you religiously practiced the discipline of the nine protocols I just rolled out. If that's the case, then you need to be ready to contend with the "S" word.

The "S" Word

Most "how-to" books don't tell you how to handle success in their particular area of expertise. It's as though they don't want to jinx things by talking about success ahead of time. I think that's balderdash. I prefer the approach of Ray Morris, my high school football coach. The day before our first game, he took the team over to the bench area on the game field – old Russ Bullard Field. "Gentlemen" he intoned, "We have worked hard. We are ready. We are going to rise victorious tomorrow night. In fact, we are going to rampage our way to victory every night this season. So the eyes of Florida shall be upon us. It is therefore of paramount importance that we comport ourselves (he was from the deep south where they love such words, delivered with extra syllables on each vowel) as champions both on and off the field." For the next 30 minutes he did a humorous but meticulous tutorial on how to conduct oneself on the sidelines.

In short, he was showing us how victory would feel and taste and smell. Did talking about victory jinx us? We lost a heart breaker the next night. --- But we won all the rest and ended up Conference Champs. So all in all, I think talking about success ahead of time is a good thing.

What exactly is Success?
In general, success is the functional completion of whatever task you set your mind to; turning a page, tying your shoes or creating new life forms on distant planets. Specific to creativity however, we'd have to be a bit more detailed. Success in this endeavor means

1. getting past the old wall, and

2. building a new one out in the meadow.

It's a two-stage process. Getting outside the old wall is only half the battle. If you don't build your own walled enclave out there, then you haven't really created anything, have you? All you've done is run away from something.

- At best you're just a talented outlaw, whose chief joy is thumbing his nose at anyone who tries to tell him what to do.

- At worst, you're the village idiot who's just doing a random walk through the daisy patch.

When does success occur?

That depends on you, really. It can't occur before you're done. Up until then you're simply "in process." So how do you know when you're done? Well, how do you know when you've gotten to Albuquerque? Is it when you cross the city limits, or when you get to city hall?

On the one hand, you're done, when YOU say you're done. You came up with the task, after all. You set the goal. You therefore should be the judge of when you've accomplished your own goal.

On the other hand, maybe the general public is the best judge. Franklin did not succeed as a stove designer until he came up with a design that the general public bought in droves, making him a millionaire. Of course, the same was also true of his invention of lightning rods. Every building on the American continent had at least one Franklin rod. At $2 a piece, he was a millionaire all over again. Or his bifocals, which half the population over 40 depended on. Yikes, there's another million.

On the third hand, if you're keeping count, maybe success awaits an anointing by the experts. Einstein was not a success until the scientific community admitted their inability to disprove his theories. And his big moment came in 1919 when an impartial 3rd party used a total eclipse to confirm that the light bouncing off the planet

Mercury behaved exactly as the Theory of Relativity predicted it would.

How far can I go --- Out beyond Success

Success is all well and good. But there is so much more to be had. Success is simply the validation of an accomplished task in the here and now. When the general populace takes you to their bosom and loves you for it, that success becomes fame. And if that fame lasts beyond the generation of your children, then congratulations, you have attained glory. And if they still remember your name 2,000 years later, and if they still tell tales of your life, your struggles and victories, then congratulations my son --- you have become a legend.

Here it is

In a paraphrase of Ray Morris, allow me to say, "Folks, you are going to succeed. You've worked hard. You've learned a lot. There is no further preparation you can do. Trust your instincts. The force will be with you. You will succeed. It is therefore of paramount importance that you comport yourselves as true champions, cognizant of victory's taste and smell and all it entails. So tuck in your jersey and get in the game."

Will I Get Weird?

I figure that if you're still with me at this point I can tell you something that might have scared you away in Chapter 1. It's my answer to a question I get from people when they first consider vaulting over the wall ... "Will I get weird?"

My answer, "You bet." The Wall of Rationality is the boundary of normalcy. By definition, anything that lies outside it is non-rational, and therefore weird. So if you play with the abnormal out there in the meadow, it rubs off.

You've just bumped into a major source of tension in organizations. Most executives tend to fantasize that creativity can be compartmentalized, and turned on and off at will. That way it gives its "good" stuff (new ideas) to the organization without upsetting the apple cart, or any of the apples that lie therein. Managers fantasize that a creative person should dress and act just like everyone else, perceive the world just like everyone else, and have the same values as everyone else. So at the same time that managers are encouraging people to be creative, they also tend to discourage them, because they squash any attendant behavior that's outside the norm. In short, many executives demand that their employees vault the wall without really vaulting the wall. A track coach who tried that approach would be fired as a health hazard.

The Hot Chocolate scenario

Back in the day when such a question was relevant, I assigned a paper to my product development class at University of Virginia on, "Which system stimulates more innovation: Capitalism or Communism?" You can imagine the responses from a group of young republicans (which most business students tended to be). As it turned out, the day they were due happened to coincide with the day the leading seller of hot chocolate mixes wanted its VP of product development to unveil their newest innovation to the press, using our eager young students as a back drop. He came. He presented. He bombed. After a breathless presentation on the development cost and process, and the expected growth of market share and profits, complete with 4 color slides and sound track, he ceremoniously whipped the cover off the little product pyramid on the desk and – TA-DA – revealed that they'd changed the shape of the marshmallows.

TA-DA. $3.2 million spent on marshmallow research. Silence. Eventually one of the young republicans raised his hand --- "Doc" he began, "Can I rewrite my paper?" Not surprisingly, the story never saw the light of day. The threat of yanking advertising dollars had a chilling effect on local journalists. What got squelched was a heated defense of what the students called "mickey mouse toro pooh-pooh". He said it was as creative as you can get in a corporate setting.

Portable Walls

When you get creative, you don't just vault the wall and wander aimlessly out there in the meadow. You either move the old wall or build a new one ... especially if there is a bunch of you being similarity creative at the same time. Then something interesting happens.

The old wall of rationality that surrounded the concept of womanhood said a woman had to cook and clean and nurture children, not business ventures. But after a generation of womanly "weirdness", that's no longer the case, is it? The definition of what it means to be a good and useful woman had changed, hasn't it? At least in public. Someone moved the wall.

The point of all this is as follows. **Being creative will make you seem weird at first. But as your "weirdness" continues, the rest of the world will catch up to you and you'll no longer be considered weird.** In fact, at some point in the future, you may even be seen as an old stick-in-the-mud traditionalist.

The moral lesson here is this:
stop wasting time trying to fit in.

We all get a little goofy when we're being creative, and even when we're not, we still look a little weird to the folks back inside the old wall. Accept it. It's the price of making your mark in the world. It's also a badge of honor. As George Bernard Shaw said,

> "The reasonable man adapts himself to the world; the unreasonable one persists in trying to adapt the world to himself. Therefore, **all progress depends on the unreasonable man.**"

Have we heard that somewhere before?

The individual
The individual is the crowning glory of creation and the veritable engine that drives society down the road to progress. Yet it's easy to lose sight of the individual in today's world, where everything seems to revolve around the group. It is especially tough for the individual to get his due in this day and age because we live in a world of false modesty. Steven Jobs (the founder of Apple Computers) and Bill Gates (the founder of Microsoft) are two of the few creative people who happily blow their own horns, and a lot of people don't much like them for that very reason. Society prefers to see the self-effacing genius who always gives the credit to someone else. That's why the world was so comfortable with Johan Sebastian Bach, its most prolific composer. He started each composition with the invocation, "God grant me the wisdom", and ended it with "Sola Gloria Deo" (To God, alone, be the glory).

But don't get side tracked by Bach's statements. They were not false modesty or the result of a diminished self image. You see, down in his gut, Bach knew that he was the only one God spoke to with this extraordinary message of music. He therefore knew his importance as an individual, and he knew the importance of honing his skills to the peak of their potential. He was just giving honor where it was due.

We Live in a World of Change

Now here's a comforting thought - that great idea you had last year is probably obsolete. At the very moment you are reading this section something is occurring in a laboratory, or out in the field, or in world events that will change things so radically that the knowledge you have at this very moment won't be enough to cope with the new situations you'll face. For example, when I started writing this book:

- Only two geeks in California knew who Bill Gates was, Ronald Reagan was President and Pope John Paul II was a vibrant middle-aged man. The internet was a tedious but useful way for academics to send binary code to one another.
- "Russia" still meant the entire empire of the USSR instead of its largest republic, the iron curtain was still firmly in place, and the Berlin Wall was a functioning wall not a series of concrete billboards or souvenirs.
- The Savings and Loan industry was still considered a viable financial player, not a $700 billion albatross around the nation's neck.
- Drexel Burnham not only existed, it was one of the most feared, envied and admired financial houses in the world.
- American Motors was an independent company, not a subsidiary of the Chrysler Corporation. And Chrysler Corporation was an independent company, not a part of Daimler-Benz (so now it's back to being

independent anyway). Sometimes change can't make up its own mind.
- ◆ Cigarette smoking was not the mark of Cain.
- ◆ There was no Amazon.com or eBay, and people got their books the old-fashioned way. They borrowed them at the public library. And if you googled somebody you were literally baby-talking.
- ◆ George W. Bush was a lightweight party boy living off his Dad's contacts and spending most of his time at the ballpark. And Barak Obama was a big fish in a small pond, editor of the <u>Harvard Law Review.</u>
- ◆ Steve Jobs was a vibrant young man instead of being mostly dead.
- ◆ People still ate junk food and babies still wet their diapers.

In a few short years, most of that changed. Thank goodness for soggy diapers. It's nice to know that some things are eternal. The point is that the world will continue to change, and if you're trying to use last year's techniques in the 21st century, you'll be in trouble.

The Simple Tasks in Life

As useful as creativity is on the grand stage of world politics and economics, don't ever forget that it's equally as useful on the mundane tasks of everyday life.

- ◆ You can change your fortunes in courtship by redefining the situation. Instead of a grand hunt, make it a dance.
- ◆ You can improve your effectiveness at work by learning to relax, working smarter rather than harder.
- ◆ You can improve your relationship with your kids by taking an inside-out approach to the problems that arise.

- And you can speed up the process of cleaning fans by realizing that scrubbing is not the only paradigm. All you have to do is vault the wall and discover that soaking is a better way to clean.

Ah yes, the fan. We've come full circle, haven't we. Creativity is like that. It leads us on a grand tour from the mundane to the divine, and back.

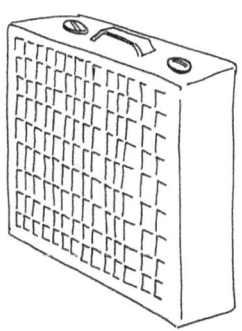

A Final Farewell

There have been two hidden players in this book - von Clauswitz and the Orient. Old General von Clausewitz wrote that war led most nations into one of two traps:

1. using the weapons and tactics of the last war, or
2. copying the opponent's tactics in the current one.

The first trap is one of obsolescence. The second is one of stupidity. Your opponent is better at their own tactics than you could ever be, and they've had time to figure out ways to counteract them if need be.

And that leads us to the Orient: especially China, Japan, India and Korea. The Japanese are great managers, with a higher ability to manage communal efficiency than our culture allows us to have or exercise here in the States. The Chinese have seemingly unlimited raw materials and manpower. India <u>does</u> have unlimited manpower – and a vast number of them have been educated in our best schools. No nation understands what makes the US and Great Britain tick as well as India. They are the vast sleeping giant. The Koreans have proven engineering skills, and together, the Oriental cultures tend to have a willingness to sacrifice individual gain for communal gain, which is definitely NOT an American trait.

As a result, the Orient can beat us on price and take enormous chunks of market share --- if we let the battle be fought on the battle ground of efficiency. We fell into that trap back in the 80s with the Japanese. They kicked our butts for almost a decade. To our credit, we worked our way back into the game, but never did more than hold them off in a stalemate. Then the dot.com era dawned and we swamped the Japanese by leapfrogging past their finely tuned technology. Nobody cares about the world's best buggy whips when there are no more buggies.

Yet, U.S. firms are falling back into von Clausewitz's second trap – trying to beat the opponent with their own weapons and tactics. In other words, we're letting the opponent decide where the battle is fought. That's why we're back to our old love affair with cost cutting efficiency – including shipping jobs to New Delhi, Mexico and the Philippines. And it will lead us down a deceptive spiral - going broke ever more efficiently.

America isn't real good at efficiency over the long haul. We're big, noisy, sprawling, brawling, self centered individualists who get sloppy and wasteful. We lack the tradition, taste and culture that the rest of the world takes for granted, and we are often our own worst enemy. We hardly ever agree with each other, and it seems like we're always jockeying for position in some strange political game of one-upmanship.

In fact, the only thing going for us is that we do two things better than anyone else.

We're more creative than they are, <u>and</u> we're more effective than they are.

When we put our minds to it.

If we want to hold our own in the future, we might want to change our tactics and build on what we do best. It goes back to the core of American business culture - good old Yankee Ingenuity, the search for effectiveness, which requires equal parts creativity and courage. And all in all, that's not a bad combination.

So go be wonderful at something. It doesn't matter what. Just be wonderful.

You now have permission.

Sola Gloria Deo

The Author - *Joe Anderson,* PhD

Joe has served as personal advisor and counselor to more than 60 CEOs, controlling over $8 billion a year in sales and 3,500 employees, in large measure, via his chairmanship with Vistage - formerly known as The Executive Committee (TEC).

He's been doing that job since 1995, along with occasional public speaking and a pretty fair amount of writing.

Prior to that, he successfully ran an organization himself, then went to grad school to find out why it had gone so well. He emerged with a PhD and taught for 10 years in some of the leading business schools in America; getting voted Professor of the Year at several of them. You can reach him via:

www.joeandersonphd.com

www.ingramcontent.com/pod-product-compliance
Lightning Source LLC
Chambersburg PA
CBHW062155080426
42734CB00010B/1693